The Poetry Review

The Poetry Society, 22 Betterton Street, London WC2H 9BX

The Poetry Review

The Poetry Society, 22 Betterton Street, London WC2H 9BX
Tel: +44 (0)20 7420 9880 • Fax: +44 (0)20 7240 4818
Email: poetryreview@poetrysociety.org.uk
poetrysociety.org.uk/thepoetryreview

Editor: Wayne Holloway-Smith
Publisher: Jane Ace
Editorial Assistant: Astra Papachristodoulou

ISBN: 978-1-911046-45-5 / ISSN: 0032 2156
© The Poetry Review & The Poetry Society, 2023

Cover: Alvaro Barrington, *When I was just trying to feed my daughter / Coogi* (2021, detail)
© Alvaro Barrington, Courtesy of the artist and Thaddaeus Ropac Gallery, London. An unwavering
commitment to community informs Barrington's wide-ranging practice. He has said 'When you look
at my paintings, you're encountering parts of my identity. I grew up in a culture where it was really
about erasing hierarchies, where we're all participating in cultural production.'

Cover quote by Eric Yip, see p.32

SUBMISSIONS
We welcome submissions. Guidelines available
at poetrysociety.org.uk/thepoetryreview

ADVERTISING
To advertise in *The Poetry Review*, visit
poetrysociety.org.uk/thepoetryreview or
contact Ben Rogers on +44 (0)20 7420 9880,
email: marketing@poetrysociety.org.uk

BOOKSHOP DISTRIBUTION
Central Books, 50 Freshwater Road, London
RM8 1RX, UK. Tel: +44 (0)20 8525 8800
or visit centralbooks.com

PBS OFFER TO POETRY SOCIETY MEMBERS
The Poetry Book Society offers Poetry Society
Members a special 10% discount (plus postage)
on books bought from poetrybooks.co.uk
Contact The Poetry Society: +44 (0)20 7420
9880 or membership@poetrysociety.org.uk

SUBSCRIPTIONS & SALES
Individuals UK: £40 / Europe: £55
Rest of the World: £60 (delivery by airmail)
Single issue: £10.95 plus postage.
Order online at poetrysociety.org.uk/shop

Subscribe to the digital archive of *The Poetry
Review* at exacteditions.com/thepoetryreview
The Poetry Review is on sale in leading
bookshops. It is also available on audio CD.

The Poetry Review is the magazine of
The Poetry Society and was first published in
1912. A subscription to *The Poetry Review* is
included as part of membership of The Poetry
Society. Views expressed in *The Poetry Review*
are not necessarily those of The Poetry Society;
those of individual contributors are not
necessarily those of the Editors.

Charity Commission No. 303334.

The Forest Stewardship Council (FSC) promotes environmentally appropriate, socially beneficial,
and economically viable management of the world's forests. By buying products with an FSC label you
are supporting the growth of responsible forest management worldwide. *The Poetry Review* is printed
with vegetable-based inks. Surplus inks, plates and printing blankets are recycled.

CONTENTS

Poems

Natalie Shapero	Oh Boo Hoo	7
	Black on Dark Sienna on Purple	8
Jos Charles	Three Sonnets	9
Caroline Bird	RSVP	12
	Downer	13
	Ants	14
Sanah Ahsan	lullaby	17
	How do you have pleasure	18
	to be held	19
Dawn Watson	Queen of the Sticklebacks	20
Kim Addonizio	Existential Voyage	23
	Self-Portrait with a Statue of	
	Fernando Pessoa	25
Padraig Regan	*Four Torsos in the Fitzwilliam Museum:*	
	GR.94.1937 (Apollo Sauroktonos)	27
	GR.2.1891 (Dionysos)	28
	GR.18.1891 (Eros)	29
	GR.1.1887 (River God)	30
Katherine Horrex	F.A.O. Granada Studios	31
Eric Yip	Broadway Cinematheque	32
Sarah Hesketh	Sunday Father	33
Helen Mort	Consequences	34
Cortney Lamar Charleston	It's Important I Remember That There Is No	
	Universally Recognized Definition—	41
John Challis	Night God	43
	Cathedral	44
Charlotte Geater	dissection after surgery	45
Courtney Conrad	I Want to Come Back	47
Inua Ellams	Unrelated Incidents. 1981	49
Jessica Traynor	i'm lydia deetz and all my friends are dead	54
	monstera	55
	and the girl inside me	56
Tife Kusoro	I keep having dreams about	
	beating up my dad	57
Luke Kennard	Fishing with the General	58
Deryn Rees-Jones	Let's Say	60
Michael Pedersen	Parklife	62
Asmaa Jama	sympathy for ishaq	64
Kathleen Ossip	Wallace Stevens	66
Momtaza Mehri	Utterances Shared Only with the Dishwater	
	She Sinks Her Hands Into	67
	At the Market, Amman	68

Rebecca McCutcheon	Bear Country	69
	Blood is Thicker	70
Prerana Kumar	Saraswati on Ritual Honeymoon	71
Jack Nicholls	For the Cat Found Naturally Mummified	
	Under St. Patrick's Church, Toxteth	73
Victoria Kennefick	Watching Your Egg Crack	74
	I Do An Egg Cleanse Because I Must	75
Moniza Alvi	The Handwriting of the Very Old	77
Sophie Robinson	*from* mother o' pearl	78
Alissa Valles /	On Zuzanna Ginczanka	82
Zuzanna Ginczanka	Explanation in the Margin	83
	Instead of a Rose Petal	84
	Firebird	85
	Vocations	87

A Mutual Uncertainty

A Mutual Uncertainty   88
Mimi Khalvati and Eve Esfandiari-Denney

Gallery

| Nina Mingya Powles | Slipstitch | 101 |

Essay

| Jeremy Noel-Tod | Magic Papers | 112 |

Reviews

Clare Pollard	A Sort of Net	118
Vidyan Ravinthiran	What Will I Do in the Future?	123
Alycia Pirmohamed	Organisational Structures	129
Astra Papachristodoulou	Excavating Language	134
SZ Shao	Poets with Guts to Spare	139

The Geoffrey Dearmer Prize 2022

The Geoffrey Dearmer Prize 2022   143
| JLM Morton | Lifecycle of the Cochineal | 145 |
| | Beetle, c.1788 | |

EDITORIAL

Shortly before the launch of the Spring issue of *The Poetry Review*, my GP referred me to a specialist for an MRI scan, with the concern that I might be facing a life-altering illness. 'It might be Multiple Sclerosis,' the GP told me, 'or it might not.' As someone who suffers from acute anxiety, I am prone to the need for certainty – a tendency to want to 'know' everything, for sure, all of the time. As such, I began daily to produce narratives around this worst-case diagnosis and how I would deal with it – as a parent, partner and poet – in an attempt to assuage the uncertainty with which I was grappling. 'Try not to worry,' my friend who is a practising surgeon told me over the phone, 'it could just be peripheral neuropathy.' 'Try not to worry,' my girlfriend told me, who has no medical expertise at all.

*

It may have been because of my present circumstances, but when reading for this issue I seemed to alight frequently upon uncertainty as a particular value or poetic concern. In the second in the series of intergenerational discussions, Mimi Khalvati states that in writing poetry 'not knowing is what is required of you', as she and Eve Esfandiari-Denney investigate the properties of not knowing, working towards a new vocabulary of understanding illness, cultural identity, relationship – to the self, the reader; in letting go of fixed and determinate meaning, the latter suggests, 'we offer the reader a parcel of enigma for them to dive into and find the truths beyond whatever we intend to say.' Often, it appears, resisting that need for an exclusive certainty, a fixed, finite meaning might lead us to articulate a deeper, richer perception and connection.

This, as a practice, seems born out elsewhere by Andre Lorde who, speaking of her childhood, in conversation with Adrienne Rich, states, 'When someone said to me "How do you feel" or "What do you think" [...] I would often recite a poem, and *somewhere* in that poem would be the feeling'. It's that somewhere I'm interested in. Not a specific word, or definition, but the searching for an emotional place to land. Nina Mingya Powles is seeking a similar place in her beautiful sequence 'Slipstitch' within these pages – somewhere between memory and object.

I began to discover uncertainty everywhere, in the poems I was including here: sometimes with humour – 'It's honestly cute that you think // you know what's coming', declares Natalie Shapero; sometimes it's feared, as Victoria Kennefick attempts to ward it off with an egg cleanse. It's distinctly present as the gum sticking together the fragmentary pieces of Inua Ellams and of Helen Mort, and at the forefront of Deryn Rees-Jones' attempt to find (or abandon the possibility of finding) logic in illness. Each poem, in its own way, makes a virtue of what Jack Underwood calls, doubting the 'finality, and the general big-bearded Victorian arrogance of certainty as it seems to appear in other forms of language'. The only certain thing in this whole issue might be my assertion, right now, that there is a glut of work here, by names you might recognise and others you might not, for you to enjoy and engage with.

*

The specialist with whom I was engaged was a very nice man, who empathised with my situation, and after examining me, suggested that I probably didn't have Multiple Sclerosis or another life-altering condition – it could, he said, be a momentary issue which would right itself, it could, he said, largely have been exacerbated by my underlying anxiety 'turning up the volume on my nervous system', he didn't know for sure.

Wayne Holloway-Smith

NATALIE SHAPERO

Oh Boo Hoo

Five years on a research study
to unearth why former conscripts wouldn't
talk about the war. It turned out
to be because nobody wanted to hear it.

Have I told you I like your flashlight?
Your trusty one gallon
of water per person per day on the bottom shelf?
It's honestly cute that you think

you know what's coming. Have I told you
about when I died and came back
and everyone begged me
to please stay dead? It wasn't, they promised me, personal –

they'd just gone all out on the funeral, and they didn't
want all that money to be for nothing –

Black on Dark Sienna on Purple

I do enjoy beholding the rectilinear pictorial output
of abstract expressionist Markus Yakovlevich Rothkowicz
at the Museum of Contemporary Art in downtown
Los Angeles where the wall text provides not only the artists' places
of birth but also their places of death Giacometti

in Switzerland Arakawa in Manhattan we play a game
where we try to guess how everyone died based on where
they died Chris Burden in Topanga Canyon whenever you die
in a canyon in southern California it kind of sounds
like you got murdered but maybe die anywhere

and it always kind of sounds like you got murdered even
or especially a studio on East 69th Street the artist
Hedda Sterne born Hedwig Lindenberg in 1910
responded to news of Rothko's death WHO WAS
THIS MAN, MARK ROTHKO, WHO KILLED MY FRIEND?

JOS CHARLES

Three Sonnets

i.

We'd loved each other, made careers
of loving, loved ourselves, and each other,
to death. Every floor was a bed
and we'd pine and we'd pine.
We were a child like a child
with a balloon, or a camera,
like a camera a man is holding.
Like a broom handle we
held the day. Like a
woman holding his
hand like a cam
era like a child
the sun cast a
way.

ii.

I gathered what wither
ed. One example, it's
not a good example
I wanted to show
you a poem with
out occasion
to climb off the
page to come
out to show
(&c.) once
hubris with
out pejorative,
and the beach would be Jurassic,
and representation, sound or referent, we'd know, an informant.
No need to list our routine extinctions. A fig somehow at your lip.

iii.

I will not wash the cattle in the cornfield of the page.
I'll turn circles in the shower and won't declare a single war.
When I could not empty myself enough I ripped the filling out
and let an oyster shell split my tooth in two, and I went to graduate
    school, for the healthcare, I admit,
and they tore it up by the root, and I turned 32,
and I met some people I liked and some I didn't
and I fell in and out of love and was diagnosed
and misdiagnosed and went on and off some meds
and saw some things no one else could see and I had my addictions
and I got up and down and real down
and broke and quiet between my laptop
and sheets and some had died and I held to what I could
and everywhere Los Angeles grew.
One day, all this will belong to you.

CAROLINE BIRD

RSVP

Uncle Stan has a lung thing.
Linda has a bladder thing.
Stew has an outcropping
of gangrenous fantails.
From a height, Jim's rash
resembles a 1922 postmark
and Lucy's nasal corkscrew
has dampened her bon viveur.
Since Mike's yo-yo diet,
his bicep has crumbled to crepe
paper and his teeth are tree-lined
with cabbage specks. Lance
spends his nights slow-waltzing
with a visitation, outside
the potholes brim with rain
like looted blisters and no one's stomach
can hold so much as a water biscuit.
A backstreet surgeon jimmied Jen's
liver open with a penlid now
she's flatspoken and wallpapered
in plum blossom bruises but
don't worry, she's dead-
set on designing the orders of service
for your wedding on Saturday
and everyone will be there
except Gerald who found an ancient
paintball lodged in his left ventricle,
intact; the doctors say
it's holding him together
but he can't risk dancing
to 'Build Me Up Buttercup' for fear of it
splattering inside him like a bullet

made of blood but he sends
forty quid (enclosed) and wishes you
a long and happy life together.

Downer

After his resurrection,
Dad was constantly exhausted
and all of his anecdotes were about soil.
He'd start a story with
'When I was dead...'
and everyone would groan.
It's hard to eat spaghetti carbonara
whilst discussing the nutrient-rich properties
of a corpse, especially when
the speaker keeps nodding off
mid-sentence then resuming with a start
like an animatronic fortune teller
with ill-fitting batteries
programmed purely to depress you
and we told him as much.
'Shut up, Dad, we don't want
any more of your soil stories.
One more soil story and we'll wish
you were dead again.'
He thought for a minute,
'I could talk about rhizomes?'
'What's a rhizome?' I said,
hoping for something scary or mystical.
'Creeping rootstalks in the...'
'Don't you dare say soil!'
Sandra slammed down her napkin, incensed,
then fled to the kitchen
to bury her ugly sobs in a tea towel.
'Now look what you've done!'

but he'd fallen asleep
with his fingers in his ears
as was his strange new habit
as if we were the boring ones,
too consumed by our polka-dotted teapots
and satirical webisodes
to appreciate his tales
of indistinguishable muds
which had no doubt
enraptured the worms.

Ants

The cereal cupboard is alive
with errant mannerisms
like droplets of coffee in space

shaped like the dark apertures
of tiny keyholes.
Truant crochets

who bunked off their orchestral scores
to avoid being reduced
to one note

and now silently roam the octaves
of tin and shelf
with no idea who they are.

I fix the crevice nozzle
to my vacuum cleaner
and switch it on.

Come on, you shrunken comet-tails.
You mincing motes.
It's harvest time.

I open the cupboard door
like peeling back my scalp
to catch the lost neurons

and one by one, I pick them off.
Each laid bare and manic
like a toddler's scribble

made sentient by a tab of acid.
Think you're safe under the cat food?
Think again.

It's kinder than poison, I tell myself,
picturing them still alive
in the hoover bag

upside down, hysterical
in the roaring dark.
And just when they think I'm finished

I come back for the stragglers
until my cupboard is clean
and my mind is in order

and I can finally leave
to collect my son from nursery
yet all the while I'm thinking

under the skirting boards,
a tin I didn't check,
the survivors are

fizzling, cold with relief.
They reunite by the Cheerios
to recover the bodies.

High and low, they search
an empty battlefield.
Not even a blackened smear,

an eyelash of a leg. It's as if
the sky just opened
and sucked their comrades in.

They hold a meeting,
speak pheromonally
of the rapture

when the blackhole opened
and they were not chosen
but left behind, wingless,

to continue in a Godless land
where lawlessness now has
the upper hand.

SANAH AHSAN

lullaby

a fistful of hair
my mother tore
from my scalp
leaving little
open pores
to gather
around dried blood
she gave for
god's corrections
slogged for what
she believed
was best for us
her palms hell's
hands how they raised me
to hurt worse
i kissed them
like any child would
the fire waiting
around my forehead
      flushed with her father's heat
my tiny, trying mother would
sing punch
      lullabies in urdu
      a 3ml spoon of calpol
      me trusting the sweetness
the words   god heals

How do you have pleasure

when you're pricked with shame's hot rake?
The stench of shai'tan and post-sex pourri.
To You alone we cry for help [1:5]. The queers
are quietly killing themselves.

White makes a muslim of threat.
Dogma makes a threat of queer.
A lie has a way of remaking itself.
In a tidal dream our gentle prophet *(pbuh)*
kisses the pearls on my brow,
Khadija takes my lover's hand
fills it with pomegranates

and says

Sit. Eat. There is more than enough love.

to be held

i tell my woman
i don't want to be
alive i'm not sure
if that means
i want to die or
i want to belong
to forever
the violet dream
of death is merely
the dream of two
unrelinquishing arms
don't we all just want
to be held my lover
places a warm mug
into my two pleading
palms is god
piqued by every
prayer – to be alive
is to be a burden
to someone
the sky skins
itself to give
a little rain
don't we all just want
to be absolved
my suicide note is singing
with apologies
fragile hope
that death unfurls
forgiveness like a
bouquet of maggots over
a white sheeted body

DAWN WATSON

Queen of the Sticklebacks

Last month, the Executive pulled a fast one.
Everyone in our street was told to move.
Builders returned in skipjacks, dropping anchor
at the post box to implement their grand plan
of kitchen extensions, updates and renovations.
It was goodbye and goodnight to everyone's homes
and wallpapers and door handles and carpets
and windows and fake tile linoleum. Overnight,
the people of Ashfield Gardens were exploded
like a stone tossed in a bucket of sticklebacks.
They had to go live in old and empty houses
on the opposite side of the stretched-out street
until the unexplained renovation was complete.
They were told it might take a year, or forever.

The Housing Executive builders wore spacesuits
to tear down my bedroom walls. When he was alive,
before my parents split, my dad painted the walls
with every cartoon character he could think of.
He thought I'd like them better than wallpaper.
And I did. Pluto, Goofy and Mickey are quare smilers.
They smiled all day and all night, even when he died.
Even though they knew as well as I did my dad
would never be back to touch up Donald Duck's beak
when I accidently tore his nostrils off with sticky tape.
The NASA builders piled up technicolour rubble.
There were bits of white feathers and red shorts,
buttons and a black circular ear dumped in a skip.
I watched while treading water.

North Belfast never used to be a whole river.
When I was small, it was a gutter trickle.
It started raining when my uncle knocked our door
in late November the year before. I answered,
and the orange-brown leaves got winched
off the trees by light that bent the branches.
He told me my dad had cancer in his liver.
I was told on the step he had two weeks to live.
It was like he said Billy Duddy's sweet shop
sold orangutans. It was like he said the leaves
on the trees were Maltesers. I lost the bap
a wee bit. I asked my uncle, What is a kohlrabi?
What is a Romanesco? I laughed and laughed.
I stared at the ceiling with my mouth open.

Two days later in his Mount Vernon flat, high-rise,
I asked my dad if he hurt anywhere. Listen to me,
Nell, he said. Remember you are as good as anyone.
Don't let them tell you different. Have a geg, love.
Make sure to cut your hair as short as you want.
And tell your future girl I said look after you.
The rest of the afternoon, we watched Formula One.
I noticed the big, black tyres were rippling.
He told me to choose a chocolate bar from a bag.
I took a Twix. The wrapper was wet in my hand.
The next day, my dad was dead.

Last summer, I stood on a chair as he taught me to gut
pike we caught in a secret lake, the slippery parcels
of innards snagged in rock-dark blood. He held the flesh
skin-side down in the frying pan with two wet fingers.
The fish bones struck a stern curve on the worktop.
He said, Very good job, Nell. Watch that wee knife.

They buried him on a Saturday. The big wake
was at my aunt's house on Skegoneill Avenue.
I saw his white face through a crack in the living
room door. The coffin floated to the hearse.
The crowd in Brantwood Football Club cheered.
Its blue metal turnstile creaked and whuppeted.
The marsh ground under the pallbearers' feet
was thick with flip-flop pike.

The grass river stretched wide to the horizon,
to the crest of a hill where the water thinned.
Rusted metal benches were sunk at angles.
Sycamore stood at the edge like stuck pins.
It was all sky and cold and river. I pushed
my bike to the top and stared out at the docks.
Fat cargo crates in pine green and ultramarine
were locked in a stare-down with the gantries.
I rang my bell to set its thin *cling-k* echoing
over the dark water, to the neck of the dry dock.

KIM ADDONIZIO

Existential Voyage

Maybe you'll understand this life when you slam
your fist into a cloud. When you're lashed to the mast
listening to the songs of space aliens
trying to dash you on the rocks of hermeneutic texts.
But probably not. Let's eat too much and drink
our faces off; anything else is a waste of time
although time is also hard to understand,
maybe made of quantum bits but maybe not,
flowing or passing, maybe an arrow, maybe
a total delusion like believing in griffins
or lasting justice for the poor.
Parmenides and Heraclitus forever at war
about the nature of reality. Are tensed facts
or tenseless facts ontologically fundamental?
I don't get it, either. More tequila? Hold this lime
while I pour salt into my navel.
Lick, shoot, suck. Quark, lepton, boson.
Teeny-tiny invisible neutrinos.
At least the ancient Greek gods
let us see them occasionally. I don't see
how anyone can cleat hitch their life to prayer.
Who do you think is listening—
maybe a great glowing abyssopelagic snail
or the single resident of Monowi, Nebraska.
So how, wondered the lonely philosopher,
counteract the omnipresent nil?
Camus suggested suicide was rational,
but to exit thus is to forever to have slain
the hearts of those you've left behind.
Better to enlist in the employ of snowmelt
or slime yourself to a sepal,
transmute the base metals of your anxieties

into a giant rose-gold sestina. To remember
that not despair nor a dearth of taxis can last.
When the cargo shifts, the boat may list,
requiring heavy lifting before it can be righted.
When you lose sight of the shore,
the sea will take you where you need to go.

Self-Portrait with a Statue of Fernando Pessoa

I could die any minute, so why not drink myself into cerebral hypoxia,
a state of impaired consciousness characterized by a marked diminution in the
    capacity to react to environmental stimuli,
is one of those questions no one has yet answered to my satisfaction

Another is, since life is briefer than a squirrel orgasm, why don't I just go to Lisbon
& stand beneath the statue of Pessoa that wears a book for a face until I resemble it,
which is another way of asking, Why am I wasting my life sitting here hating my hair

I could at least be lying in a hammock on someone's farm
& writing about butterflies & the golden shit of cows
But I don't really care about butterflies, especially when they land in poems

& I don't want to estheticize shit either
though I'm okay with Francis Bacon pointing to a pile of it & using it as a metaphor
    for life
which is something I read once on a card in an exhibit of his paintings

Maybe "life is shit" is a good enough reason for starting in on the tequila
even without the unpromising coda
Añejo is waiting in the cupboard above the stove like a WWI recruit

about to be dragged out & thrown into a trench waiting for the guy next to him to die
so he can have his rifle, because there aren't enough rifles
In a war death may wear you for a face, & someone else can describe it

I mean if you're actually in it, not joy sticking a drone & strung out on Jack & Red Bull
I mean if a mortar splashes onto your stove or the roof of your bus
I mean thinking about war makes me want to drink myself into a state of impaired etc.

Then again I've never been in a war so why am I being so morbid
Sometimes my brain takes a thick *Guernica*-coloured Sharpie & scrawls all over the
    scenic view
& it helps to spill something with at least 11–14% alcohol on it

Pessoa was a pretty morbid person, often terrified & depressed
He wrote a poem about dying young, & he died at only 47—of alcoholism
"Only" means I'm older than he was when he died, sick & tired of almost everything

Sometimes I just want to go someplace quiet enough to hear my bones grinding together
Then again maybe the world isn't terrible & I just need a different leave-in smoothing
    conditioner
A compact folding home treadmill to get me moving again

I shouldn't ask for so much from life
Even butterflies sometimes have to dine on urine & turtle tears & rotting corpse ooze
while I've got a nice Sancerre with a hint of stony minerality chilling in the fridge

Maybe I'll take a trip to Portugal & pour some on Pessoa's tomb
& when I die—did I mention it could be any minute—you could visit me
& remind me of how beautiful it all was

PADRAIG REGAN

FOUR TORSOS IN THE FITZWILLIAM MUSEUM

GR.94.1937
(Apollo Sauroktonos)

Like driftwood
was my first thought –
which was not so wrong: him being,
too, a consequence of slow erosion, & fetched up,
here, a continent away from the mountain he was
first excavated from (that is, before he was a he,
before the gross stone of him was forced
into this imago of soft muscle). But
it is not the abrasion of his outer
layers that you notice first, their
reptilian patterning – & not
the yellowish clast opening
on his stretched left breast.
It is the fracture of his hip
that returns him to the purely
geological; it is his curved gestalt,
extravagant as a hermaphrodite.
It is his abnegation of shape that
makes him pure gesture: a spurt
of stone, unburdened, almost,
of everything that might
reduce him to a person.
Flying over it,
in fact.

GR.2.1891
(Dionysos)

I've seen your head; or, what I should say is, I've seen so many heads, exhumed

like swollen roots, that could make their homes in the vacant space above your broken neck,

where, on this one day – of all the days I've come to look at your python-thick

remaining leg, your monumental chest, the shallow crater of your navel framed

by your abdominals' parentheses (which almost are, but are not quite,

like the real enough to let me think that underneath this pitted stone whole biomes

go about their work of breaking other bodies down to rebuild your own) –

at this time, our position in this hemisphere, this hemisphere's relative point

in both its orbits, whatever atmospheric quirk dictates to the clouds

the fugitive structures they, for this moment, are & are inhabiting, & who could

possibly count how many other improbable things have all aligned

to let some sun spill through, which your pretty head, were it still attached, would occlude, though

your back, with its three cracks like a fish's gills, would still bristle in its shine;

I can't regret the choices that have brought me – little supplicant – here before you.

GR.18.1891
(Eros)

(traces of wings remain

on his back) reads the text

appended to this bone-white

foot of stone,

like an apology

for forcing onto him

this burden of a name

he never asked to hold

or to be held within.

& so I bend my neck

as far as the glass allows

& see two milky folds

pointing, like labia,

their faint, sloped arrow

towards the contrapposto

hummocks of his ass.

There is an old idea

that before we were condemned

to the sexed body, we lived,

eight-limbed, two-faced, complete;

& that what we call love

is just our best attempt

to repossess the double

nature of ourselves.

This is the opposite

of what he represents.

He is the hole the self

is built to mask, & can't.

GR.1.1887
(River God)

you could be the Colorado | you could be the Seine | you could be the Tiber you were lifted from | you could be yellow, red, blue or green, or the totality of these | which amounts to the same as their total absence | you could overspill | & if you did, who knows what prayed-for growth might come as a result | you could flow (not only as a trope) | the curve of your spine could be some bowed meander of the Thames | your muscles: the rippling of its surface (which, like yours, is only metaphorically a skin) | your legs could be diverging shores & the space between them either mouth or lough | your crotch could be a harbour perfect for a market town | &, yes, there is something islandish about the rounded slopes of your chest | an algal canopy could bloom on your exterior & choke whatever hair-fine plants might happen to be wafting in your depths | innumerable fish may well have pushed themselves along your length to dump their gametes on your rocks | you could be nothing but a joke about permanence | (our interminable reaching after it) | & the truncation of your limbs must not be understood as an indictment of the things we've done to water

KATHERINE HORREX

F.A.O. Granada Studios

It would be as banal as falling for a middle-aged constable.
If not at first sight, then at some point during his several hours search
for your would-be assailant's knives. Noticing the hair on his forearms
while he ghostwrites your statement. That it forms a sparse, dark grass.
How his brogue bends an extra syllable into the word 'wedge'.
That he lists your profession not as 'writer', like you said, but 'housewife'.
As banal as you to send – via the constabulary – an invite for coffee.
Then finding him, as you wheel your bawling toddler up the hill,
with this letter in his hand, talking to the father of your child.
An inspector telling you, over the phone, that you need 'a cold shower'.
That there's room in their holding stalls if you need to spend the night.

ERIC YIP

Broadway Cinematheque

In *Yi Yi* a boy's camera shows people the
back of their heads. In *Happy Together* two
men tango on the other side of the world.
After the movie my mother tells me she is
divorcing my father. We are sitting in a
seventy-year-old cafe near closing time one
floor above Temple Street. The tiling is
composed of repeated octagons and squares.
Accordion blinds filter streetlight onto
turquoise tables. If I were a cinematographer
I would want the shot to be from outside
looking in so my face would be half-hidden.
In *All About Lily Chou-Chou* a boy listens to
his Discman in a waist-high paddy field. This
is after the trip to Okinawa with his friends
where malevolence first enters his life. What
life one has yet to live is a question one
should always pose themselves. The milk tea
is cold and she cannot finish the luncheon
meat and egg sandwich. In *Farewell My
Concubine* a mother chops a finger off her
son and sells him to an opera troupe. Posters
cling to the cinema's white facade above the
ebb of moviegoers. Someday you might walk
in and find a story already holding your
sorrow in its hands.

SARAH HESKETH

Sunday Father

Because the last thing I wanted
was to have a *special talk.* Or to pass
uninterrupted hours at your bedside
trying to come to terms. So when
you do confide you've *no regrets,*
it's surprising how much I want to
slant my head and say, *Really?*
Not a single thing? Not even that time
we set out for Accrington looking
for what you said was Britain's
largest collection of Tiffany Glass?
It often rained on Sundays, and
I want to remind you now of us
sitting in car parks, listening to
Meat Loaf; the cracked music of us
singing *Two out of three ain't bad.*

HELEN MORT

Consequences

you met me
under London Bridge Tube Station
in a cave of purple light
a rat crossed the floor slowly
you wore brown leather
I was awkward in my new coat
you picked up a pool cue
I took the evening's hand
and the consequence was glancing
and the world said   *be damned*

*

a man called –
          (met, followed by an adjective)
a woman called –
at a bar in the stopped
heart of London
he wore his smart shoes
she wore her face like a curse
he rolled a cigarette
she ran backwards   arms open
and the consequence was unheard of
and the world said   nothing

*

a man
met
a woman
underground
to drink black sambuca

black jeans
she wore his smile for days
he did –
she did –
and the consequence was
the world

*

and the consequence was a night bus
and the consequence was a room
with a white travel kettle fastened to the desk
and the consequence was your tongue
my hummingbird legs   my shaking ribs
and the consequence was the moon
        how so often it had the measure of us

                                        (on a night bus
                                        you redrafted me
                        the engine shivered at the traffic
                        lights)

*

you were sleeping on sofas
I was an oily feather   wind-lifted
we met
we met
to hold each other at the edge of England
you wore the imprint of a hand
I wore my hair pinned back severely
you were years away
I got the first train north
and the consequence was almost touching
and the world said   *leave it*

*

you were me
I was –
we met predictably
in the song's bridge
you wore the River Humber
I wore my grandma's favourite perfume
you did a thing with your eyebrow
I held your name in my mouth
          until it fizzed
and we carried each other's sentences
and the world the world the world
said   *oh well*

*

you wore my fingers on your collarbone
I wore your stubble rash on my thighs
you wore the taste of me for miles
I wore a halo of smoke afterwards
won't take it off for anyone

*

(he said

          she said

                    on the seashore)

*

we met in all your old haunts and found them still haunted
you carried me like a mug of very sweet hot tea
your breath on my earlobe was enough
you knew where I was in a room without looking

*

you were a picture
of the waves breaking at Withernsea
brown water   white foam
a rock-like texture
though it makes no sense
to find mountains in the sea
it's there, subtle,
you   to   me

*

you redrafted me –

               (a cormorant
                   on the River Don
               widow of flotsam
               and frothy scum
               lone hunting
               like the magnet fishers
               like
               try keeping us
               apart)

*

and the consequence
was our bright diagonals
your eye open next to mine

saying meet you in static
in the hum of traffic
in a snowglobe where we're still

turned this way and that
letting it all
fall down on us

*

and the consequence was your ideas, my skull
and the consequence was a skylight
and the consequence was
            falling entwined
from the slenderest branches
landing like buttered toast

*

you were –
you met –
on avenues that belong in oil paint
you wore nothing-but-the-best-for-me
I wore someone else's silver
you flicked ash into the dark sea
I hovered above my own body
the long haul flight of it
and the consequence was lost on us
and the world backed off

*

do you want to see me?

                                        like water
                                        quivering
                                        on a leaf

*

I was late
you were on time
we met in my hometown
to watch it gentrify
under steel-coloured clouds

you wore a cigarette tucked in your beanie
I was spilled ink everywhere
we walked past the saw manufacturers
you were the passport photo in my wallet
I couldn't sleep for weeks
and the consequence was quickening
and the world said   *time, please*

*

because we were side by side ecstatic
we forgave the yew trees
we clawed down the moon
just to skim it across water
ripple ripple sink

*

on a night bus

                              on a night

                    you redraft   redraft

                                        redrafted me

*

(a white phone box
          heron-stately
makes the light through it
seem bleached
you pass
imagine you hear it
ringing   think
hello think

is that really you?)

*

bus shiver

bus shiver

bus shiver

stop

*

you met you
I met me
on a sage green duvet
in the last frost of the year
you wore my skin
and I wore yours
you took my lip in your mouth
I took your word for it
and the consequence trembled
and the world said something
we can't catch

CORTNEY LAMAR CHARLESTON

It's Important I Remember That There Is No Universally Recognized Definition—

but   I prefer to theorize it as

        empire pointing inward
or   *gravity's pursuit of the sparrow.*

        I tend to measure it

by the bloat of the city budget
and the boom it buys the cops to play with.

        I often read about it

in books that I pulled from a trash can
fire in the park nearest my apartment.

        The thread that holds a flag together.
        An assembly line that makes dog whistles.
        A light bulb over a brain dimmed on its right side.

It is impossible to write authoritatively about it
unless you are the authority and thus
have no intention to address what *it* is.

        Violence without violins.
        Truth as the shadow of the lie.
        The monopoly on I.

Nobody agrees with me on the meaning
that wouldn't also argue particulars and process:

knowledge in the prison of a school;
God in the prison of a church;
citizen in the prison of a criminal.

You can never define a word outside a context,
and the life we are suffering is context
enough to say it, prior to it pronouncing itself
the only way it knows how, a hard way
allowing the lesson to be learned too late—

the loudest silence comes
after the loudest are silenced.

JOHN CHALLIS

Night God

At first, we don't believe, so quick
we hardly make it out between the streetlamp
and the willow, but it's there again
against the dusk, feasting over bloom and rot
all insects are heir to while children
hopscotch on the pavements, climb gates
and fences into our partitioned habitats,
the concrete yards we sow and seed or abandon
to the creepers, it's all elbows and propelled
as though struggling from a chrysalis,
a sentence part way through the saying,
reborn through its hunger, swallowed back
into the air before you can say its name,
so quick, we don't believe, at first.

Cathedral

From now on, god will be the one in need of us. Screaming little god
passed from breast to arm to breast, asleep wherever sleep begins,
red-cheeked, barely dressed, attune to any movement, then up again
in tears demanding arms to fall asleep in. We stand above her, tall and
dark at any hour, alert as towers at this birthplace of our faith.

CHARLOTTE GEATER

dissection after surgery

if i said no.
if the coil.
if it bit me & hung there.
where did so much blood come from.
if i found sesame seeds in my coffee.
if i was still bleeding.
if the blood spat.
dry as wicker worked
in summer. if the silver nitrate
cleaned me dry.
if its alchemie made me new.
if my cycle was religious
as the full moon &
not always looping further
from me. if sex cured
cancer. if the ultrasound technician
put the tube inside me.
if i threw up eight glasses
of water & had
to drink them
again.
if my ovaries were alive.
if no part of me
could speak. if the medical
incinerator ran backwards
and all the discarded parts
of us came back again.
if my womb had thumbs.
if my cervix wore a hat.
if kissing was enough.
if i'd not worked myself
through the desk & into

loam & bone fragments.
if eating well made me sick
& starvation made me
better. if my body
was still mine. if i'd never
been too tired to read.
if i'd never given up
the pill. if i'd never slept
too much for a regular
schedule. if i never bled.
if i never tasted blood.
if i'd had a baby young.
if i never left. if i never
met any of you.
if the speculum didn't hurt.
if sugar rained from the sky
& coated my hair.
if water poured from the ceiling
& never stopped. if it poisoned me
& i was allowed time to recover
or die. if my body
was a birthing pillow.
if i could walk to the marshes
& back. if i could hold down
a job. if i had thumbs
for eyes. if i didn't know
what had been cut.
where did the hospital begin.
if there was never so
much blood again.
if i started to shed my hands
& face. if i opened up
in fresh water.
if the pain was the whole payment.
if i ate oysters & fries all summer
& sat on the grass
& watched the castle inflate
tiny bodies moving inside

COURTNEY CONRAD

I Want to Come Back

as Paris Hilton's teacup Chihuahua. My
home, a luxury Spanish colonial-style
mansion. King-sized bed accommodating
my morning sprawls. Maids awaking me
with a butt scratch and a hot towel wipe
down. In the background Real Housewives
of Calabasas Dog Park on a 97-inch TV.
I'm no cruel boss. I gift my maids a tip: a five-
minute bathroom break. Chef presents a
platter of salmon avocado toast with chia
seeds and a champagne flute full of sparkling
water. Driver pulls the limousine around
with a police escort for a day trip to Rodeo
Drive. My body never touches the pavement.
My shopping assistant's forearm is a chaise
longue. The purse with my magic credit card
tucks into the suit pocket of security. I could
walk out without paying or being searched,
but I like seeing the six figures, the card swipe.
A Cadillac collects my shopping bags, only.
I return home to my masseuse waiting by
the poolside, my happy ending: a cucumber
water and grilled chicken Caesar salad.
My travel agent books a private jet for me
and my golden passport, a random change of
scenery is important. Meanwhile, I meet my
therapist in my guest house for additional
privacy, you know how cleaning staff can be,

or maybe you don't. I'm sorry, I'm working on reminding myself that there are people out there less fortunate than myself. I practice gratitude in the basket of my bicycle. The midnight air, a gated lullaby. I can't even imagine it. Dying like a dog.

INUA ELLAMS

Unrelated Incidents. 1981
#After Tom Leonard

1.
Isoko is
the language
of the bush
he said
the language
of the bush

Well
I don't speak
Edo
she said / hand
on her hip
like
a sheathed
knife

when we have them
we should teach them
the language
of the
intellect
the tongue
of the learned
is English

Then when
the door slammed
shut / he raised
his head
to nod

in silent
agreement / flung
out his right
foot boldly
from the bed
and smiled

Fine / English
it is

2.
If you still
haven't
worked out
the difference
between
what is right
and
what you want
leave me
alone!

If you still
haven't
figured out that
sounds of words
have power
if you haven't
realised
our kids will

inherit
the historic
wahala
brought to us
all those years
ago / well
my stubborn
husband / as
God said to
Adam

in the womb
of the garden
of Eden
I don't care
what you think
leave my fruit
alone

3.
This is the
six o'clock
news the man
said and
the reason
I'm speaking
English is
because when
the British came
they dismantled
our natural
communication
channels / sold
our historians
and teachers / killed

who resisted
lumped together
hundreds
of tribes /
their five hundred
languages and dialects
into this pressure
cooker of a land
mass / called it
Nigeria
and shoved the King
James Bible down
the throat
of the southern
and middle belt
at gun point
leaving relations
with the north
in tatters / but
their tongue secure
This is their
legacy / This is
the six o'clock
news /
Listen up

4.
Sitting guzzling
a bottle
of Guinness
Foreign Extra
Stout / humming
the first line
of George Benson's
'Greatest Love

Of All'
in time with
the bare-chested
village drummers
Happy as
Larry / you
might say

the husband
was turning
over the
possibility of
cracking open
another
when Omo
the champion
the Jaguar
threw
the great Nosa

Omo turned his back
and Nosa pounced
thinking this
a crack
in the champion's
defence

Omo sensed
the shadow fleeting
over the soil
of the wrestler's
circle / turned
plucked Nosa
from the air
in one
movement

and slammed him
to the ground
so hard
the whole
country
shook

5.
At the grand
theological
football match
between the
orthodox
Kano Bombers
and the
trendy
Bendel United
wahala
erupted when
a young trendy
afro-headed student
told a fanatic
in a full
kaftan and
Zannar Bukar
that he was
in a flagrant
state of
religious
confusion
to which
the kaftan
replied /
Why don't
you shush

your mouth
and watch
the game
in peace /

It's not
a game
she replied /
neither am I
watching it
I'm here to
witness pure
battle / my faith
over my heart
before the ref's
meaningful
symbol / for
the ref
above this
ref / to
which the kaftan
replied /
you're talking
rubbish
woman / that
is a load
of piss

Miraculously
it started
pissing / and
in the spirit
of Pan-African
unity /
the pair sat
giggling

watching
the field flood
under the one
secular
newspaper

6.
It was caused
by us civilians
the mother
asked / And
officials being
too greedy /
her manager
replied / not
enough
transparency
all lining
their pockets
and misuse
of foreign
reserves to
revamp our
economy is why
we led the coup
d'etat / Now
we've got to
pull in
our belts
and our backs
or stay this way
you've got to
admit it

Then he cracked
his bottle

of champagne
open / poured
a pint's worth
in a glass
half filled
with ice and lit

his cigar /

a Cuban

7.
Despite
the fact
that she
belonged
to a
tribe of
people
who had
had their
language
mocked
since she
was born

Despite
a long history
of poverty
and the
violence
of people
in positions
of power
telling him

his muslim faith
was a sign
of his
intellectual
inferiority

this for
the purpose of
instilling
self-hatred

amazing
as it
might seem /
this
ordinary
working
couple got
up one day
and
were heard
to remark
that

it wasn't
such a
bad time
to raise
a child

JESSICA TRAYNOR

i'm lydia deetz and all my friends are dead

    thanks for welcoming me to the circle
i didn't think it would end up like this. even though
    i asked for it by wearing a veil
(demon thirst trap). by hanging around
    this older man. i swear he had charisma.
ok. he saw me like no one else ever
    saw me. even if that means he saw himself
in every mirror i looked into.
    someone has to mind the strays.
girls are so afraid of maggots. grave worms.
    black eyes.
but I'm still here and I'm getting better.
    a lady in the chelsea market
read my aura, said to trust my instinct, not my brain.
    how do i know which is talking? i asked.
the instinct won't negotiate, she said,
    the mind and its problems are all this red tulle –
she stroked the flanks of my wedding dress –
    this indigo light at your throat is the truth, she said,
running her fingers along my rope burn.

monstera

mum tells me i climbed up a wall of shelves to eat it and she thought i would die
      swiss cheese plant   lacquer-leaved threat
        i tasted curd in my mouth every time i spoke
             longed to pack my mouth with cheesecloth
      until breath was a whistle in dry caverns
the wet in me all sucked away   oh my lost monstera
        guard the shadows of our house   haunt the corners
           twine your arms around me   as i lick your poisoned wax
i'll take the chance to practise
        i've years of this ahead of me

and the girl inside me

slides out and jerks up on her legs like a wet foal,
falls over for a man and drags herself through the streets
rattling like a string of cans
sweeps up leaves and dirt and pigeon feathers
in her hair

and the girl inside her slides out and makes a perfect dismount
but she staggers – and there's broken glass – studding her legs – for this
man you see –
and she's a car siren you can't knock off

and the girl inside her claws out
through pondweed   turf under her fingernails and she's roaring   but
over she goes –

and the therapist says *I just*
want to stop
you there you know
that trauma isn't all that's passed on –

roaring I continue and over
she goes
over she
goes –

TIFE KUSORO

I keep having dreams about beating up my dad

I google what it means
that he's giving birth in the bathroom of the community centre.
He refuses an epidural. We argue about the gaps in his spine.
About my girlfriend. About whether it's appropriate for me to
check his cervix with my fingers or shut my eyes and use a stick.

He's planting a beanstalk, climbing to God.
While I'm stuffed in a bindle on his shoulder, breathing through a hole.

We're cartoons, drawing each other in the margin again.
I'm angry that he's always here. He's sad
that I've only given him one shoe.

LUKE KENNARD

Fishing with the General

The General did not read fiction or watch films or television. As a matter
of principle. He tore the crusts off a slice of bread and squashed
the middle into a pebble which he threw into the water to attract
carp. Carp! And it was not that he couldn't be *bothered*, I was to
understand, but rather that he thought it was *morally reprehensible*
to care about, *to be made to care about*, someone or something
which didn't exist.

We, who existed, cast our lines in the golden dome of dusk.

The thick grass compressed beneath our buttocks, the spring a vestibule.
In the General's memoir he will recall this as a happy evening, but
I have been sent back in time to befriend, to love and to eventually
kill the General

so that his memoir can never be written; a memoir described as *remote,
vacuous and savage* and identified as the root-ball, or *a* root-ball, of
our present difficulties.

The Department of Time approves intervention in the past only in order
to prevent or facilitate certain books being written; albeit, as the
Minister for Time once put it over dinner, a modest intermediation
which might be just as well achieved by writing another book.

This, of course, would presuppose a broad readership with adequate
down-time to read things in their year of publication.

All of which notwithstanding, these are the parameters the department
has been designated and sometimes, for a joke, we would go back
in time and cause *each other's* memoirs not to have been written,
just in time for the book launch. Hahaha!

I rifled through my bait box and stabbed my finger on the hook of a
      bright purple feather and gasped. All of his strategic victories, you
      see: it was the times that he had acted on the 'spur of the moment'
      rather than taking due deliberation, or consultation, or caution.

What's that you're reading? the General asked, noticing my line had gone slack.

You wouldn't like it, I told him. You would find it *morally reprehensible*.
      The general laughed and gently nudged me with his shoulder. It
      occurred to me, as it often did during assignments,

that I might stay here for the rest of my lozenge (we referred to our biological
      lifespans, untethered from any coherent calendar, as lozenges) and
      abandon my own time to its fate; that I might make the General happy
      and not kill him; that the General might, after all, turn out to be one
      of my supervisors, or colleagues, or *invisible adjudicators* who had
      at some point made a similar decision. I felt a tug on the line and
      arranged myself around it.

DERYN REES-JONES

Let's Say

Let's say it was a box, an illness box. A box of wrongness and betrayal. It
felt like a grave. It was the whole world. But not exactly. Let's say

I was alert, I was lost all night, I couldn't move. I was tethered. Let's say
there was something on my chest, the weight of time, an elephant, of
Memory, a strange bird, with texture like the teeth of a piano

being played,

of fallen stars smashed falling to the ground. Let's say it was a
nightmare, like *The Nightmare*. Let's say I was the ground with earth,
   like dirt, my mouth

as my blood clotted, and my lungs failed.

Let's say the weight felt like the weight of the heaviest element
oganesson
(I googled that, it lasts for just a millisecond, its protons like a blob).

Let's say I felt like a cartoon, an anvil weighted in my chest:
Road Runner, Bugs Bunny.
Let's say on the phone the nurse said, in the early hours, do you think

you're going to die, let's say I didn't know the answer which
retrospectively was good. Let's say I was on hold,

the ceiling falling in. I saw it. 111. I was speaking from my dreams
in tongues.

Let's say I couldn't breathe so I proned, let's say I really lost it, my
daughter like a small lamb, nuzzling my hand. Let's say the
prime minister was reciting the *Iliad*,

his party trick, a monster in the corner of the room. There was red wine
spilled like blood

on the carpet. There were
invisible arrows in my chest. Let's say I was

falling to the ground that It was in my nervous system. Let's say.
Let's say I vomited. I

said. Let's say

I felt, speaking into time, I felt the dark, the fourth element.
It felt that everything was collapsing
as it moved like something streaming in my veins, let's say

I felt stoned. Let's say a day begins so anything can happen.

We were on our own. All of us. Let's say there's so much fear the dead
rise up.

Let's call the day *Here's a memory like a little tear of fear.*

(I was in a taxi and
the doctor couldn't get her hazmat suit on and so for what seemed
hours I waited.

And when she came she touched my arm and held it for a while although we
    weren't allowed
to touch, and o with so much tenderness,
let's say, and

outside, later, I could hear the sirens, people clapping in the evening
there were rounds

of applause.

But no one was really listening.) Let's say I lost something. Forgiveness.
Let's say I was left. Let's say there were tanks in the streets.

Let's say I was singing, I was calling to the Furies, let's say let's say let's say
    I had never

felt so cold.

MICHAEL PEDERSEN

Parklife

a kid
        squat down on the edge
        of a kerb wonderdrunk
        from slapping a gutter puddle
        with a stick la-la-la-ing up
        towards the roof of a tree
        she can't fathom the crown of
the river kelvin
        writing scripture
        performing miracles
a feral cat
        on the windowsill of the park
        warden's cottage scowling in
        at a spoilt pet's sleeping spot
        imagining such easy dreamies
        paw prints mark the glass
the ghosts
        of snowmen
a hippy scavenger
        holding a grimy rock
        up to the light
        shaking off its dirt bunnies
        until shot through with flakes
        of irradiant opal
just a crow
        without its metaphor for grief
fox
        strutting insouciant until changing
        trajectory as if hearing carols
        in the distance & deciding
        to track them

a black bench
      with your name on it
an old can
      of irn-bru wibbling
      on its bars
      come to think of it
      it's just like
the gloaming
      to make everything appear
      more tigery
            how quickly we come out
            of the moment how long
            before it truly lets us leave

ASMAA JAMA

sympathy for ishaq

armless god my brother wants to be drowned
head in turpentine and weeping
he wants to be scripture ink lashing his skin
martyr'd
in a dream i reveal myself his mirror image, i split my areola with a razor and say:
   see, i am your blood
my wound flows and we take it as a sacrament –

we are so sanguine and soiled no mosque will admit us,
at last he sleeps – and as he does sunflowers grow from his head, unliving,
unslaughtered,

armless god reject his sacrifices
even though he wants to be drowned
head in turpentine and weeping
he wants so much
                 so much to be prophet
we speak of religion like bread
my mother hands us an oregano plant,
he wants it to bloom, so he can burn its leaves as an offering
as he sleeps

i drown it,
we wake each morning to its rotted roots – i want you to accept this in his place,
i want you to let my brother live as you let ishaq do
i want him back
i watch a bull brutalise a glass window with its forehead,
the pane shatters and shatters against it,
there is so much of it the blood,

i want him a calf again, only fourteen and asking me about wounds

an imam mentioned once, the blood that never stops flowing
the one that frees you from isha and asr,
i once let a splinter stain my sock, strawberry –
i once let myself open like a fruit, star-rot,
it was not enough i kept scabbing over
i learnt later, it was womb-split that let me splinter from the masjid, i spent all
day at the park on the swings, bleeding and free
i want my brother to join me,

let me take his place, let him sit where i was on the swing, open my knees if
you have to, fill my head with your words and take my voicebox, i can be your
good sacrifice, i can bray in his place

make me ashen, make me a tomb,
take me to the place ringed celestial, i can make nice with the winged things,
i can forget earth, spare him

KATHLEEN OSSIP

Wallace Stevens

When I read the poem about the jar I thought: of course. The jar
bosses the bushes. Tennessee's a graveyard, tidy and such.

But jars are open by definition, or if lidded the lids can be twisted off.
I climbed a hill I would rather have rolled down. I placed a lid on the jar
and twisted it off whenever I wanted. The submissive air poured in.

The preposterous speak when and how they like. Up close
unadmirable, at a distance they glimmer. The talentless lick dirt.
A homely jar without carving or ritual dancing ignores the same
things we do. Let the bushes grow.

Let go let go is a sandpaper wish like your scratchy day-old growth.
Your jar is attractive and useful; every force pushes me towards order.
I'm not ready to be fathomed. Flourish of trumpet announces a plain
mason jar. The jar's mouth has an authority like Van Morrison. Soon it
might well be a glass tower.

I can't forget that a jar contains and is labelled. It's cool performance
art to put it on a hill. It's uncool non-art that fills it with pectin to be
spread on a crust. How long will it stay upright on the hill I want to
roll down? Frank and damp the morning comes. The jar meets beer
bottles and other litter. In these surroundings, a jar cannot confront.

Dominion isn't dark-robed like you thought, or if it is there's a
handgun in the folds of the robe. A large-bodied large-headed man
should know a jar isn't gray unless full of gray matter. Juxtapose all
you want. The jar is bare, cool in my hand of glass. Compared to you
I will always be young.

MOMTAZA MEHRI

Utterances Shared Only with the Dishwater She Sinks Her Hands Into

Don't tempt me with a good time.

My final courtesy will be closing the door on my way out.

I can't leave if I never arrived.

I mopped the floor with my sweat and it wasn't enough.

They say that guests, like fish, begin to smell after three days.

I am familiar with rot.

Your grammar rules have taken years off my life.

Terror is incredibly pedantic.

No one can protect me from myself.

This country is like a husband. Its wayward children are always my fault.

My children will not come with me.

They have nothing to go back to.

The years have swallowed me.

I am like a congealed clump tethered to the sole of a boot.

I am grateful for the exposure to your superior values and asbestos.

I am grateful for what kills me.

If you paid me to leave, I would kiss your hands.

At the Market, Amman

With practised indifference, I stared at the caged pigeons.
Their breeder winked his one good eye. I stood behind you.
Your back, a shield from the naked fact of their suffering.
Not far from your birthplace, I watched the assured flight of your hands,
bargaining for something I didn't understand. And in that moment,
I envied you. You were within sight of your grandfather's land.
A knowledge swelling the distance between us. I silenced my slug of a tongue,
heavy with words I knew I would regret. My own lanes had hardly changed.
Alight here for the 168. Disembark for the maternity unit where I first nudged my way
out into the republic of northwest newborns. Out, out, out, into the world,
first like a tease, then all at once. Bloodied and beatific.
Out, out, and into the shadow of the Mother, where I remain,
steadfast in my doubt. Brushing your fingers, always accidentally,
I cross a hospital's threshold, of a memory mine to mine,
but for someone else to recall. Still a stranger to where I began.
I pluck a village from my grandmother's throat. Dress its bones with prose.
I have a right to a home I can ransack. You have no right to your ransacked home.
You straddle the limits of a country you called a holding pen for your scattered people.
Each fleeting indignity confirmed this.
The laminated identity documents you carried.
The gleam of corrugated iron in the sun.
Born to teenagers who chased each other through camps, you dangle in the interim.
Language pitches the tent. I stretch the category to fit us both. I fail.
I fail. Later, on your bike, I curled around you like a starfish,
tracing the ladder of your ribs. It must be a sin to want more than this.
To hunger for the crusted dirt of a beginning under my nails.
Yours could never be mine. I spoke your language.
You could not speak mine. I haggled for mercy.
All around us, the feathered fever of imprisonment lingered.
The smell of it would not leave you.

REBECCA McCUTCHEON

Bear Country

At a cookout in the mountains we're talking about bears
firelight reaches through the dark for our faces.

The evening lasts for miles. I used to see maps and think
London was made of stations surrounded by empty space.

Canada is really like that. The creaking owner of the ranch
is talking about two things I've only seen in North America:

guns and smores. He is made of silver lines and serious looks
covered in the country. Heat melts the marshmallows, licking

their corners black. He takes a bite. The intention goes off
silently. Things are always softer in the middle. My mother

says you never see stars where we are, but I'm sure I have.
If it's dark enough you can see Ursa Major from anywhere

in the northern hemisphere. My thoughts are at least three
conversations ago. *If one came up here, I'd have to shoot.*

All I can think about is how long a barrel must be to end a bear.
Doubt is such a giveaway. *Yes*, he says. Without hesitation.

Blood is Thicker

I'm running away and the river helps. Greenery blurs.
Focusing on each leaf is migraine territory. I'm boxing

up my own plans in favour of my brother's, conducting
suicide watch by text. How our parents made us share

our worst parts, when we haven't done the same things
not stayed in the same hotels, not been black-eyed

by the same boys – just sat together on the backseat
of an argument, complained about the babysitter

caught a French mouse in a saucepan. You have to be careful
who you mix with. What the plans are. How the other

side of the bed holds a dog. I want to live closer to ground
than the roof will let me. On the stairs this morning

I faced our father, wrapped like wet meat in a towel
knowing all there is to know and all he can say is he doesn't

remember where the carpet went, that he wants acrylic paint
for Christmas. Wasn't your favourite colour always red?

PRERANA KUMAR

Saraswati on Ritual Honeymoon

Imagine throwing up for four hours
on the bus ride

up those breaching hills, and anthurium season!

buds teething along the road's limits,
their lips grudged open for honeydew

Imagine the bile cradling your stomach,
amber tides refusing to lull,
even when the road unreels and stretches
its hot asphalt stamen, dusted
in sacred daikon powder

> If this is a warning, you are a fresh goddess just birthed
> out of a navel

> Nobody told you

And he buries your acrid plastic bags
at rest-stops till nightfall, brings back fresh
plastic; first touch crackling
between your thumbs
as you rush it to your gurgling

If you are grateful,
it is because he is smiling
gently while he does this

Here are the many bride-things your mother has wrapped for you –

lemon-smeared novels,
an ornate waterpot, marigolds
circling the budspout,
the family's larynx rosary coiled inside, strung together
on squirrel guts

Bloodmarks to help suture your prayer,
cast into sacred mangroves at dawn
for succour

If it leads back into your calves,
your guardian severed the lotus roots
nestled in your heels while you slept

Nobody told you

At night in bed, he brings you a bouquet of pickings –

a score of anthuriums, threaded
with plastic needles, tissue clods,
a rag you'd used to wipe your mouth

Look at my nails, he says on top of you,
dark brown slivers pressing
his offerings into your blushing face

None of us heard you
say yes

Imagine me as an egg in your womb,
thawed and just released, still shy
to the membranes of my shuddering world

If this is his entrance,
I can still taste him digging
into your mouth,
frozen in half-bloom

JACK NICHOLLS

For the Cat Found Naturally Mummified Under St. Patrick's Church, Toxteth

So first the earth collapses and you drop
into a darker dark, an older chill,
the air inside your stomach hard and still,
and later, voices call for you, then stop.
Then muddy panic falls into the cells
you dream of blue tits with, and panic smacks
its skull against your skull and hopes for cracks
and underneath, the drying mouth expels
a PLEASE MIGHT SOMEONE HELP inside a shout.
At last, you pick a place and disappear.
Your body fortifies, becomes a crypt,
a vault inscribed I WISH I HADN'T SLIPPED,
a little leather purse of I AM HERE.
Hey cat. I see you in there. Please come out.

VICTORIA KENNEFICK

Watching Your Egg Crack

If the egg was a lightbulb
and the lightbulb glimmered above your head,
shining, bright, yolk-coloured,
a beacon, lighthouse in the dark
and then the light, the yolk, the glass,
cracked
and flooded, trickled, tinkled, crumbled
down so you were covered in it,
new or something,
present or something,
oh my god,
real or something
and the lights all over the house winked
and my tiny, tired heart jolted too –
such voltage
such a shock
      a shock
             a shock.
Darling, why are you so fucking shiny?
Why do you blind me?
Pieces, pieces, everywhere,
on the floor,
in my hair.
Who has been hiding in there?
Folded up like a box in a box.
Nowhere for me to fit,
just goop everywhere, albumen,
the chalazae cords, the useless
fucking embryo.

I Do An Egg Cleanse Because I Must

You might do an egg cleanse if you are feeling a bit off.
I feel unlucky and sad. I do an egg cleanse.
In a bowl I clean the egg of any negative energy,
add a spoonful of salt, then a squeeze of lemon juice.

I wash it gently; I say a prayer.
Please help me, please help me, please.
I rinse the egg and dry it with a towel,
it's as bald as a baby so I cradle it.

Next, I fill a glass quarter way up
then hold the egg in my hands,
it warms and I blow my intention
onto it, all the things I'd like to get rid of.

With this cleanse I free myself of bad energy!
With this cleanse I will no longer have rotten luck!
With this cleanse I will make the right decisions!
With this cleanse my life will return to me as it was!

It's time to sit down then. Holding the egg in one hand
I rub it along the back of my head, then to my ears,
and my hot, tired face. I close my eyes and smooth it
along the lids, across my lonely lips too.

I go from head to toe –
the egg is taking it all away, the bad energy,
the mistakes, the delusions, the incessant weeping,
the feelings of helplessness, the rage –

time to crack, into the glass goes the yolk.
I wait for things to settle
and peer through to see the shape of it,
the colour oozes to fill the container.

Smelly water or blood: there may be evil spirits around me!
Bubbles: negative energy was absorbed into the egg!
Cobwebs in the whites: I may have an evil eye on me!
A face in the yolk: I have an enemy!

It doesn't matter what I see, or which way I look,
because even though I beg for grace and
frantically search out for space,
there is still so much egg on my stupid face.

MONIZA ALVI

The Handwriting of the Very Old

My mother's faint and hesitant words
are like bird prints in the snow
only just reaching their destination.

Her hand shakes slightly, she's breathless.
The ruled lines on the notepad help her.
Is my own handwriting smaller now?

My stronger lenses magnify it.
All this printing in the snow – I ask
the wind to carry me across the distance.

SOPHIE ROBINSON

from *mother o' pearl*

i.
Little things. little things move
me the most. always have. keep me
in your pocket for the rest
of your life. tuck me in your bra. little
things fuck me the most: folic
acid tab dissolving under
my tongue; blood in my toilet you
were only a little thing. dot. i am
only trying here right now to set
the scene. *this is me trying.* o don't
set me on the ground, walk away
& forget to come home. don't drown.

i've been drowning my wild moods
on my therapist's couch & one dull
cloudcore afternoon
she asks me how it feels
to be nobody's first priority.
i bite the cushion i'm bracing
my chest against, twist the corners
of my teeth against my cheek
until i smell blood. at home
i scream into the cat & leave
the lamps off & let the light
go, night pouring in the window.

love pours down the edges
of *this mess i'm in* and out
again & by july the heat is unholy
& makes us sadder *all*
the flowers that you planted

mama burning on the edge
of the city the forest pumps
a black layer of cosmic
grief into the atmosphere
& the cars won't start &
the dogs stop barking *all*
died when you went away.

some nightless nights we away
ourselves from the city & wade
into the river moving carpets
of bouncy algae with long strokes
of our arms, our chests bobbing
atop the jelly thick water towards
the railway bridge, empty trains
thundering overhead & swelling
waves of heat wobbling the air
we gulp on the underside. a sign
above us reads HALLOW WATER
& i think this life is wasted on me.

months earlier: i waste the time
i have between the moment
you died & the train i'm waiting
to catch towards the empty
space you left around you.
i cry into the phone my sister
holds the other end of a hundred
miles away & light candles & let
the internet rot my brain until
day breaks. when i walk out the door
sucks shut behind me & i gasp
in the holy air of your breaking.

ii.
I am trying to break each day
open like an egg on the edge
of myself; to be the day's
empty space *slide into me*
that way one more time & i
swear to god i'll in my child
hood homer simpson beat
his son & nobody was okay
inside. bro do you even pray
that one day things will feel
different
          physically i'm on my knees
emotionally i'm lying down.
down the road you're a corpse
in a hospital mortuary. i dunno
what to do w that fact so i set
it down bc it's heavy & hurts
me as i tread down the path
to the end of your garden.
on the lawn it sits big and still
watching me weep in a dead
man's shed, googling *can my ancestor*
come back as an egg i laid inside me
can i get what i want yet
can i get what i need now.

all that week i needed to believe
in something more than i believed
in how dead you were. dead dead
the word sang itself like a second
heartbeat. five or six or seven of us
crouched in your house each day & held
your wife against us like a frightened rabbit
& when i sunk my arms to the elbow
in the milky dishwater each night i gagged
on your goneness & my sloppy impression

of your careful habits & mistook my sadness
for a sign like you always told me not to.
tell me not to be so sad this time i ask
whenever i hand you a shallow cup
on your way to the bathroom. after you go
i hold the cup between my thighs & tear
open the sterile wrapper around a small
syringe often used to feed kittens
milk or shoot medicine to the back
of a baby's throat held open
in a scream. the cum coats the cup
like mother of pearl & i know it knows
things i don't. i suck it up tilt my hips
to the sky & imagine myself a life.

my aunt texts me a picture of the sky
over your home the night i've left:
the full pink moon. *moon where the streams
are again navigable. moon when the ducks
come back. moon when the geese lay eggs.
sucker moon.* i turn my phone over.
earlier, in a train toilet, i had pissed
on a stick & prayed over a swelling
red wave, closing my eyes
against a single line & longed to be small
again, to have never seen my father
cry, to have never felt

                  my pelvis make a fist.

ALISSA VALLES

On Zuzanna Ginczanka

Zuzanna Ginczanka was born Sara Ginzburg in what was a revolutionary city, Kiev, in 1917 and raised in the town of Równe/Rivne, now Ukraine, by a Russian-speaking grandmother. She made her poetic debut in Warsaw, by then the capital of an independent Poland where, in the 1930s, lively literary movements and quarrels thrived alongside a growing tide of political extremism and violence. Her wit and beauty made Ginczanka a dazzling presence in the editorial offices of magazines such as *Skamander* and the satirical *Szpilki*, and at the tables of café Ziemiańska and Zodiak; however, after publishing *On Centaurs* in 1936 while technically still a student at Warsaw University, she did not have much time to build a body of work before being driven into flight as a Jew under the Nazi occupation. She lived in hiding first in Lwów, where a Polish concierge betrayed her to the occupation authorities, and then Kraków, where she was found and executed in 1944 or early 1945. She is most famous for her last poem, 'Non omnis moriar', a parodic testament that turns a famous Polish Romantic lyric by Juliusz Słowacki on its head, denouncing her denouncer and symbolically bestowing her 'Jewish things' on those she imagines looting her home after her death. Her natural bent as a poet was toward passionate exploration of the physical and intellectual world and of the Polish language itself, made to sing and think in ways that strike readers in Poland now as astonishingly new and strange. After languishing in oblivion for half a century after her premature death, she has in the last few decades been recovered, published and honoured by a new generation of readers, scholars and artists. She is a poet of anticipation, a poet of the future tense with all of its excitement and anxiety. In a very short time span, she achieved in her best work the powerful fusion of sense and idea embodied in the title of her first and only book, inflected by the stark tragedy of her times.

ZUZANNA GINCZANKA
translated by Alissa Valles

Explanation in the Margin

I did not rise
from dust,
I will not turn
to dust.
I did not descend
from heaven
and I won't return
to heaven.
I myself am heaven,
like a glass vault.
I myself am earth,
like fertile clay.
I haven't fled
from anywhere
nor will I return
there.
I know no remove but myself.
In the wind's swelling lung
and in calcifying rock
I must
find myself
as I am
scattered
here.

Instead of a Rose Petal

My tiny city has a few too many streets
(I count them all daily, yet we never meet).
My tiny city has a couple of streets too few—
(but not one for a meeting of just us two).

My tiny city could stand above a thousand
of the sort whose sidewalks run on and on
and each with millions of slender dwellings,
people crawling ant-like like pits in melons,
—each different everyday filled by your love
could ring the bells of meetings over the roof,
over houses like a giant piano's colored keys
—and we would walk
without end
and in us there'd be peace.

My tiny city could stand on a short mini street
just the one and only, as narrow as a creek,
and that little street could have just two houses
facing each other, laughing bells to rouse us—
we could go out from our houses in the evening
or in the morning: laughing, joyful, springlike,
and meet right there, hand-in-hand hearts ringing
and gaze into each other's eyes
without end
without end
as long as we both would live.

My tiny city has too few mini streets
and a few tiny streets in excess
of what I could guess ...

Firebird

I don't know my fulfillment as I don't know my death.
Amid what sandalwood trees and among what angels,
bracing its vocal cords with the tongue's wise sting
does Firebird with flaming feathers call and disquiet?

Under a zoological sky the breathless animal park
marries a lion's star sign with an ardent live lioness;
I run through lovers' groves. The earth stirs to flight,
the sky slowly falls. They will meet at my lips.
Will a wing strike me here and dazzle my eyes with light,
where June, burning rose of winds, budded and bloomed?
I run, alert, and look: in the grass, girlish girdles
and sharp-shooting bows of hunters in another lost chase.
My love saw and chose me—and here he strides like a
       lion:
"A ship sails today, to tenderness, it waits with raised
       banner!"
In vain. I know: I will not go. Not yet here, not now
will the birdsong smother my breath like molten lead.
For there's a flapping of wings. Dreams' flutter and fright.
A feather lost in flight tickles the soft moon.
In the distance a protracted gurgle. The call. And again
I don't know my fulfillment as I don't know my death.

The chase leads me from green lovers' groves into battle,
the Firebird with its feathers unfurled circles over the field,
commanders check their armor, scenting honor and glory,
I cover my face with a visor in mind of knightly customs,
and draw my heavy sword—my eye circling upwards.
My indomitable chief races, scattering enemies with his
       voice:
"A ship departs for victory, it waits with resonant
       banner!"
In vain. I know I won't go. Firebird plunged me in a cloud.

I raise my visor sleepily and go, conscious of my losses,
into the still, frozen underground, full of subterranean
memories and dreams wafting from walls. Exhaustion
crushes my throat, and I trail a harsh wake of poems.
In quarries of sorrow I disavow birds and fulfillments,
I touch a column of basalt; "Lord," I repeat, singing—
"try me with grief, despair, the pit of ruin and death
but don't try me with happiness; I won't stand the test."

But suddenly—a flap of flight. I think I hear a far voice,
I run back into the green moist grassland, and again,
bracing vocal cords with the tongue's wise sting,
Firebird with flaming feathers calls and disquiets.
But there is no absolute thing—and therefore no thing
can cast me into ultimate love, or ultimate doubt or rage,
the feathers' flash can't scare me, nor the song calm.

Vocations

Praising the craft of war in poems slashed by the censor,
with violent rhyme and valiant hatred of man for man,
youngsters with thighs of flint tightly bound in leather
went with a clang of greaves and terrible flash of arms.

Euphorbus stabbed Patroclus; beautifully Hector gored him,
Hector was beautifully slain by thunder-helmeted Achilles!
Sing the club and ax, the brave and double-edged blade,
the arduous dance of blows, keen foresight of resistance.

Yours is the task of judging in a forceful soldierly stanza
man's hatred for man, and clothing the verdict in a chant—
while my fiery task
is to strain in the night's cool pitchers
the resonant honey
of a woman's
different
song.

A MUTUAL UNCERTAINTY

An intergenerational discussion

Mimi Khalvati and Eve Esfandiari-Denney, in conversation

EED It is lovely to meet you for the first time. I wanted to start with a line of yours from *Entries on Light*; 'the stronger a gesture, the lighter / its recovery'. For me, this seemed to contain Persian wisdom. Even the syntax reminded me of the phrasing you hear in spiritual verse. For example, in Rumi's, 'What you are seeking is seeking you' there is this kind of chiastic proposal: here is the problem, here is the answer. The way I read your line was, 'the problem is a lack of conviction, the answer is in an aftermath'. I'm taking 'the lighter its recovery' to be less about weight and more about clarity of vision.

What I loved about this line was how you seemed to infuse a sense of 'Persianness' without writing *about* Persianness. This got me thinking about how the culture of poetry so often considers the ways in which POC or 'othered' writing problematises poetry. For example, there can be a self-fetishistic impulse to create an anthropological rather than imaginative lyric persona. I wondered how you felt being Persian has enriched your practice?

MK Yes, you've gone straight to the heart of the matter! Perhaps if I tell you where that line came from, I think that will say quite a lot about what you've just said, about reading and about othering – or about reading through a different kind of cultural lens? Or maybe just through a purely imaginative lens, or purely literally I don't know... 'The stronger a gesture, the lighter / its recovery.' It's from a very short poem in *Entries on Light*. The following line is 'On a black sea / how far the spirit sails!'

When I was at drama school, we had a wonderful movement teacher called Yat Malmgren, who was a Swedish dancer. He taught us a class called 'movement psychology', which he had developed from Laban's study of character analysis, which was about understanding psychology through body language, or the other way around if you're the actor expressing it. It was about demonstrating the psychology of the character through your relationship with time and space, and how one moves within a space. Yat taught us that if, as an actor, you make a physical gesture, such as thumping a table to emphasise a point, that is the 'action'. Then the 'recovery' will be completely instinctive, it'll be the way you might withdraw your arm, and you won't notice that part of the movement, you only notice the physical action of thumping the table. But you'll feel the fist comes back towards the body, or maybe rest on the edge of the table and how your elbow relaxes, and so on. So that line related quite simply to physical action – if you make a very strong physical action, the 'recovery' will be weightless, will be incredibly light.

I'm lingering on this because it does relate to writing, or to my writing and the way I think about writing. Yat used to say things like, 'Oh Maryam [using my original name], how light is your light? How heavy is your heavy? How direct is your direct?' And I've translated that principle into writing. Say you're writing about an image or a feeling, or whatever you're relating to. One needs to give it its exact degree of truthful weight. You don't make it even a tiny fraction more significant than it really is, or more dramatic, or more beautiful, or more anything than it actually *is*. Or any less. You have to find the exact degree of whatever quality your words are expressing.

EED What you are saying reminds me of your line: 'The sensation of an eye'. I definitely read this sentiment in your work. Also, it's interesting to now know the origin of that line and how my reading of it was so coloured by my knowledge you are Persian.

MK It's a very essential question for both of us – how do you position yourself vis-à-vis how you might be read and to what extent you might be Persianised and solely read through that kind of a lens. People might assume some sort of Iranian literary or cultural reference that just isn't there in my case, since I have very little connection with my own Iranian-ness or with Iran, or with the literature or culture. So that's something I've lived with, and to some extent battled with, since I first started writing. And I feel I still am, in the sense that what a reader might assume may simply be because of my surname or the knowledge that I'm Iranian. Is that a problem you relate to?

EED Well, I just made that exact assumption! But I do relate to my work being read this way. During my MA in Poetry at UEA even my mentioning something as inconspicuous as 'fruit juice' in a poem once triggered a class discussion on the speaker's supposed Islamic faith. This was in the context of juice not being an alcoholic drink, and therefore being 'halal'. In reality, the poem was about being lonely and a conversation on its lack of originality would have been far more helpful. Besides, I've never been to a mosque in my life, so I struggle to see when my speaker would have.

I mention this as an example of a broader issue, one that was discussed widely by POC students on the course. How could we learn when the critique of our poetry was first and foremost a discussion about race? Especially when discussions on race are so often divisive. There were also no POC tutors on the course, so navigating this huge racialised creative obstacle wasn't native to the people teaching us. Saying that, I am guilty of wanting to read Persianness into poems by Persian poets. Poetry has served as a way into a home culture I feel very disconnected from, so I want to hear from it when I read a poem by someone who might offer insight. However, I should be careful doing that, I want to be mindful of the implications of reading work in search of this sense of connection, because it produces such a specific lens, or a paranoid lens as Sedgwick would put it.

MK Tell me more about your disconnectedness – because I'm more interested in disconnection than in connection.

EED Well I was raised in London, my father is Romani traveller and my mum Iranian. She passed away when I was young, so I think the contextlessness of being part Iranian then amplified its significance. I suppose this goes back to what I was saying about how being part Iranian or 'other' can enhance writing. I feel very accustomed to a sense of bewilderment regarding my race. Yet, it's become a feeling I want to embrace in order to keep wondering, and therefore keep writing.

MK That's so amazing, I love that you're saying that. We're talking about feelings of disconnection, but at the same time, making these connections – because my last book is called *Afterwardness*, and earlier you said something about 'aftermath'. The word aftermath is a very key word in the last poem of that book, and 'bewilderment' is a key word in the first poem!

When I was sent to England as a child – I was literally put on a plane when I was six and sent to boarding school – I had no English and I was always in that state of not knowing. I don't know who I travelled with. There must have been somebody or I might have just had a label, like evacuated children during the war. I have really no childhood memories of Iran at all, but I was trying to remember being on that plane and having a vague memory of it. The sensation I had most strongly was bewilderment and just *not knowing*. I'd never even been on a plane, couldn't speak the language and had no idea of what England was. I probably had very little concept of what a *country* was. So a huge void of not-knowingness.

EED That sounds deeply bewildering. Maybe it makes sense that you would then be drawn to a craft like poetry, as it does embrace the unknown. It's the perfect activity for bewildered people.

MK Absolutely! Bewilderment, or that state of not-knowing, has not only enriched my verse but it is the reason why I write.

EED It intrigues me to hear you relate to the feeling of not knowing, yet form seems very important to your work. I wondered why it is you choose to use given form? And also, how do you negotiate its certainty?

MK Before I answer, tell me how you connect 'not knowing' with form?

EED I suppose I think of free verse as a heightened context of the unknown, it's like feeling around in the dark for the shape that you need but don't know yet. Whereas given form involves some level of certainty, or a framework. You know the shape of the poem before you've written it. I'm thinking particularly using a form with a very recursive nature, like the ghazal. There is a predictability, and there's a point to that predictability. So I wondered what draws you to it alongside this sentiment of the unknown?

MK Yes, that's really interesting. There are so many paths I could go down from here, but I'd like to take a path that leads to your cottage, as it were.

I think the idea of form as certain is at once true for me and not so true. You do have, as you say, a framework. I don't want to always refer to the ghazal, because I've worked in many other forms. I've only ever written nine ghazals, but people associate me with that form. But in the ghazal, for example, the most exciting question is how you will use that refrain? You don't know the second time you use it how it will be different from the third time or sixth time. Each sonnet that you write, you have no idea how it will be different from the last sonnet you wrote. Will it be a distant cousin? Will it be a twin brother? What will the relationship be? You're always swimming in that unknown. And this is why I love using form, but I also love writing in free verse. Of course with a free verse poem, you also need to find what form it is. It's not necessarily a metrical one, or a fixed or given form. Either way, when writing poetry in general, I don't know what I'm going to say.

But that very 'not knowing', as you say, is legitimised by the space of poetry, by the fact that you're working in an art form that makes it honourable and not shameful or embarrassing. Poetry, in fact, does the opposite: not knowing is what is required of you. Because if you know too much and if authorial intention is going to just lead the way all the time, you're not going to write good stuff.

I don't know if I've quite come to your gate, but I sense that you relate to that position of uncertainty? Is that right? Is the state of not-knowingness important to you?

EED Yes. Not knowing is definitely my starting point, as you describe with your own writing. Although, the act of crafting language seems to bring me closer to a sense of certainty. I'm thinking of the nature of narrative in relation to traumatic experience. If you can assign a narrative to something traumatic, you enact putting the fragments of a shattered reality back together, you can begin to conceive of the inconceivable. I'm not searching for absolute certainty by doing this, but I'm hoping for some remote sense of logic, a version of truth. For example, I had cancer treatment for twelve years as a child, teenager and young adult, and the doctors often referred to my leg as 'the leg'. It helped me to call it that too, it was a way of confirming a loss of agency over my body, it was no longer my leg, it was behaving of its own accord. Maybe the leg would kill me? Maybe the leg would save my life? It is in this way that language can solidify a reality. It's strange, but just to articulate something, just to say it, can make something real. It's often the case we talk about the futility of language in literature, but I'm more worried about the futility of what we call reality, and language helps me decipher something human and therefore small from it.

MK I think that's brilliant, the way you have communicated something so crucial just with the use of an article. It's probably the most invisible word, and yet the import you have given it is huge.

EED Yes, 'the leg' is a truer article for a leg anyway. Whose leg was it in the first place? Although, saying this, I do appreciate the magnitude of language, and how it is such a futile tool to communicate *exactly* what we mean. But this isn't a bad thing in my opinion. Language is surely a spiritual material to work with. We have inherited it through ancient permutation, and because of this, language must hold wisdom beyond and above our use; words and phrases have more knowledge than we do in applying them. Yet, as writers we try to manipulate language or even master it to express what we mean when ultimately, by producing literature, what we offer the reader is a parcel of enigma for them to dive into and find the truths beyond whatever we intended to say. So, it's not so much that we use should language as a communicating wave of knowledge, it is instead an ever-expanding horizon of experience.

MK You express that so beautifully, Eve, and I'm so glad you can talk about language in a much less literal way than I do! I think poems in particular are themselves new events and always grounds for discovery, both for the reader and the writer. But I'm very interested in how you construct your narratives, because that's something I'm also completely incapable of doing. I've never had access to any family history, since I only went back to Iran when I was seventeen. I've never had anyone say, 'Oh, do you remember that time we went to Disneyland' or whatever, so I have no sense of narrative, especially biographical narrative.

I wrote this last book, *Afterwardness*, to, as you say, *search* for what it is to not have a story in an age when having a story is so crucial. And I wondered, what if you actually don't have a story? If you can't access it, google it, if you don't have relatives to tell you about it. And there are millions of people, I'm assuming, in that state and we don't have narratives, and we can't construct them. So how else do we give value to our experience? How do we communicate it and so on? That's what I was searching for. And what you're saying, which I totally believe, is that to construct a narrative is so essential, even if it's just one narrative, one fiction as opposed to another kind of fiction – but how do you do that? Teach me!

EED I suppose, for me, it has something to do with somatic sensation. I trust it can constitute latent memory in the body. For instance, cancer really exposed to me to the infinite nature of physical pain, there really is no cut off point. In my practice, I can ruminate on where memories of that emerge in me, then explore the dramatic effect of how that relates to language. For example, I find traumatic feeling rears its head in my having a dark sense of humour. This inspires quite a stark oscillation between light and dark in my work. So, by understanding the emotional root of my idiosyncrasies as a writer, I find myself speaking to events I can't quite remember, or even believe are real.

MK I can't begin to imagine...

EED Well, neither can I!

MK Except I can relate to that loss of memory or forgetting. For example, being at school with three hundred English children, within a year I'd forgotten Farsi and for a while I must have had no language because I hadn't yet learned English. And I can't remember what that was like.

EED Do you have a feeling for Farsi when you hear it?

MK No, not really.

EED Is there a sensation in your body when you hear it?

MK Well, I do have pangs. But when I went back to Iran, nothing was familiar, nothing. The only thing that was – and this relates to your body experience, how things are remembered by the body – was food, and the smells of food. And even now, having relearned it, I can't speak Farsi very well.

EED I see. So how have you navigated not having concrete memories... I know you said you haven't resolved it entirely yet, but how are you negotiating it?

MK I've just had to accept it. Though when I hear other people talk about their family history, with a massive amount of detail and circumstantial information, I do feel envious. The thing I mind most is that I've passed this lack of collective memory on to my children. They're not children now of course, they're coming up to fifty, and they can't remember their childhood either. I remember recently one of them said, 'Oh, you never told us anything about Baba' (my father). They didn't realise how little I knew about him to tell.

EED Yes, not having a sense of a collective memory that aligns with where you are from can involve a very strange, specific kind of mourning over what was always intangible, like familial strangers, or an idealisation of homeliness. Mimi, I have a pamphlet of yours, *Persian Miniatures*. I noticed in a few of these poems, you make the fact you are Persian explicit. I wondered where the impulse to do that came from?

MK I think it was something you yourself said, there is so much we can't remember but what we do remember, we sort of *salvage*, I guess. What

I was saying earlier about being read or misread through an 'Iranian' lens is something I've brought about myself. In a way, I've asked for it, because I *have* written explicitly about my Persian background and people have mistaken those poems for childhood memories, but in fact they came from the three years I lived in Iran when I first went back as a young adult and lived with my grandmother.

When I started writing poetry in the 1980s, there was very strong anti-Iranian sentiment in the wake of the Iranian hostage crisis [from November 1979 to January 1981, a group of Americans were held hostage following the take over the US Embassy in Tehran]. So the poems I wrote then were primarily about my Iranian family, particularly the women, who were the closest to me. I wanted quite simply to present positive images of Iranians, to undermine the stereotypes current at the time.

EED Wow, that's a big poetic ambition.

MK Well, I mean, it was just a little tiny thing I could do. I started writing when I was working in theatre and feminism was more central in my life then than cultural homelessness.

EED What you're saying is reminding me how tricky the ethics are for interacting with the subject of 'Iranian women', or even just the act of associating yourself with the 'Iranian female poet' title.

MK What do you personally find difficult about this?

EED Well, I've sensed myself benefitting from its marketability despite having such a disparate connection to Iran and its culture. However, it does feel important to name my race in a literary context. British poetry has always been about identity politics as it's a white male tradition, and, in my opinion, being explicit about your ethnicity in relation to your poetry is acknowledging a history of racialisation in literature that has always existed and still exists.

Saying this, I'm aware it can inspire fetishisation by publishers and magazines, or even be self-mythologising. But personally, what I feel overrides the negative political gesturing is when I consider the history and cultures of the women in my family, both Persian and Romani Traveller, and how little permission they had, or still have, to speak, and even to live. Yet these are the women who lead to my existence, an existence that has the dignity to write and to be read. This makes it feel celebratory to say where I'm from in relation to my writing. However, I still experience a sense of imposter syndrome when speaking on this subject poetically, do you?

MK Honestly, you're absolutely expressing it all so clearly. I feel you just put it in a nutshell. Yes, there is huge pressure on us and the imposter syndrome weighs heavy. This is why I have not written many 'public' poems on anything to do with Iran. But that brings me back to your other questions about the ghazal. The form itself seems to somehow give me permission to at least dip a toe in the water.

EED What about this form gives you permission?

MK Perhaps because the ghazal asks for certain kinds of commitment. You can't be all thistledown and lyric-y. The closed couplets in particular pressure the syntax and ask you to commit yourself to a statement. They offer a certain kind of courage almost, because they come with a rhyme and a refrain and take away the fear of sounding portentous, or pretentious, or what you were saying about that imposter-syndrome feeling. It's like the form is standing beside you, holding your hand and saying, 'Just stand here. It's okay to stand here and say your name', which of course you do in the signature couplet. Do you see what I mean? It's quite, sort of, *parental* in that way.

EED That's so lovely. The ghazal, the Persian parent!

MK That's not *why* I wrote ghazals. I started almost out of a sense of duty, because I was trying to write sonnets and villanelles, all these forms from other cultures and other languages. And I came across the ghazal and I thought, 'Oh, whoops, as an Iranian, surely I should attempt this'. I was very interested in what you can bring into English poetry through the ghazal, rather than conveying what the original is like, because I can't really read the original anyway. I think that, maybe, the space to write a political lyric, as opposed to a polemical poem, was something the ghazal did offer. But it also allows you to be sentimental or extravagant, exuberant, somehow less muted. And a bit louder, actually, because I tend to be soft in my poetry. Do you find you've also got something like multiple egos or voices?

EED Extravagant and sentimental are definitely words that characterise both the ghazal and Persian culture in my mind. And yes I do, in the same way I feel I have multiple egos and voices as a person, I suppose. I find when writing it's often my aim for their contradictory registers to interact with each other, or play together maybe. This relates to a question I had for you actually, about the longevity of writing. I was reading your work last night and wondering how you have long maintained a sense of play. Because it's something that's so important to...

MK To younger poets?

EED Yes!

MK Nobody's ever asked me that. They've said 'how did you manage to keep writing' but not referenced this sense of play, which is lovely. That's very important to me. That's *why* I do it. I don't write because I feel I have burning things to say. And I never did. When I was at school, my English teacher used to say, 'you should be a writer,' and I'd think, 'Oh, my God, how awful, I wouldn't have a thing to write about', until I realised later in life that actually nothing *is* a subject in itself. Or what I define as nothingness.

To come back to your question, yes, play is important to me. I think it is to you too? Your art is very playful – you combine the playful, almost humorous, with very dark material. It's your ability to seamlessly flow from seemingly opposite or very varied things – 'piercing a song with a pin and letting the life out', as you put it so beautifully.

But I also progress from dissatisfaction, which I think is a very strong, creative source. Dissatisfaction with my own work. Not in a miserable way but, for example, after I've written a book, I read it very brutally. And I think 'OK, these are the things you've done. Those are good. But look at all the things that are missing. What can't you do? What are your weaknesses?' I've felt my whole writing life is an apprenticeship. And I still feel like I'm serving one. After my first collection, which was the usual miscellany, each of my books had a specific objective. My second book was trying to figure out what on earth am I doing in free verse. The third (heavily influenced by Calvino's essay 'Lightness' in his *Six Memos for the Next Millennium*) was how to achieve lightness and speed. And 'lightness' is a very Iranian aesthetic quality, isn't it? I think all Iranian art has a wonderful weightless quality, maybe it's in the blood? But, anyway, it didn't come easily for me, I had to work at it! And then I did another book to figure out how to *think* in metre. And then another to extend my vocabulary. It sounds idiotic, but it is how it happened.

The first time I addressed subject matter thematically was in my last book, *Afterwardness*. And this was because I discovered a seminal work called *Third Culture Kids*. TCKs are defined as people who have not spent their childhoods in their country of origin and the book explores the after effects of that kind of upbringing. For the first time, I felt I was reading about myself. As we were saying, sometimes people make connections in your writing, particularly with reference to migrants, refugees, or placing you within an Islamic context, that you just can't identify with. But the experiences of these chameleon-like Third Culture Kids, who have little curiosity about their own stories, no biographical memory, retain no factual data from their early lives and so on – it was my own experience, all there in black and white!

EED And this was prose?

MK Yes, prose nonfiction.

EED I see. Yes, it's so productive to read something that sees you. I often find this happens with writers who can draw something idiosyncratic from what is a seemingly hyper-politicised subject. By this, I mean writers who can speak on race, class, sexuality, gender etc in ways that embrace specificity and resist clichéd signifiers that imply 'otheredness'. It's so difficult to achieve, in part because the various and intersectional representations of minority subjects have had such little air time throughout the history of Anglophone literature. I'm still unable to draw on a text that really resonates with my experience as a biracial 'woman of colour'. However, it seems what inspires my work is a reckoning with the imaginative consequences of that limitation, which isn't always a bad thing, but it's definitely difficult.

Also, it's useful to hear how prose has been useful to your poems... I'm learning how important reading outside of poetry is. I'm also learning that reading poetry can sometimes be the worst thing for writing them. Maybe it relates to this idea of maintaining play, when you first begin writing and reading poetry you haven't quite acclimatised to what a poem *is*. I now have to make a conscious effort to not lose a connection to that very initial and naive enquiry for what a poem could be. This is why it's so nice to read your work and hear you talk about your work, you assure me there can still be that lostness, there can still be an imposter syndrome.

MK You mentioned those four fatal words, 'what a poem is'! Tell me about your writing. You write so differently, and of course for your generation there are differences in approach, or maybe just differences in process, or what we think a poem is?

EED Yes, perhaps a definition of poetry is ultimately personal. For me at least, a poem is essence, or the essence of its subject. I had an amazing tutor for my BA at Goldsmiths, a poet called Jack Underwood. He taught me about poetry's *aboutness,* as in, a poem is not about a thing but about the things circling around the thing. Although, if I tried to think about this more in relation my work... Maybe I would say a poem is something as broad and embarrassing as a request to be heard? What would you say?

MK Of course, the minute you say what you think it is, it leaves you with a horrible feeling because you feel you've diminished it somehow. And I wonder, not only about the nature, perhaps changing nature of poetry, but also about the timescale and speed of writing and reading it, given that we produce poetry on different platforms now, especially social media.

EED Well, it's notable that I occupy a much faster world than the one you were in as a young poet. For me at least, poetry provides an antidote to that fastness, it operates on a much healthier frequency to how I live. The poem itself is keeping you still, asking you to wait and hear something, and writing poems involves a similar request. Also, when it comes to interacting with publishers the advice seems to be 'take your time'. Then I meet someone like you who has sustained writing books throughout many years your life, and I should mention here, it's such an honour to meet you. When do other creative industries find time for an intergenerational conversation like this?

MK To be honest you and your work really do amaze me. And likewise, this is something that my poetry life has given me. I've worked with lots of people, one-to-one and in workshops, and it has really given me a sense of the *extraordinariness* of people's lives. Although I must say, yours is really super exceptional! Not only in the difficulties that you have overcome, which is incredible, but also in the richness of your heritage. And to do this through poetry. Poetry loves particularity – doing what you're doing, making something palpable by putting it into language, defining the *particularities* of your experience and the way you've interpreted your experience. By the way, do you identify as a poet of colour, would you call yourself a poet of colour?

EED In a way that makes me feel confused, yes. Do you?

MK It is confusing. I would say 'yes' too, in solidarity, although I think both of us are trying to resist being homogenised into stereotypes that box us all in together.

EED Yes, in part because it's just far more stimulating to resist it. It's such a delicate act of poetic craftsmanship to write that balance by which we do not refuse our race, yet not feel as if we completely constitute it.

MK That's exactly what I meant about the particularities and the nuances. When you ask me about my writing involving my Iranian family, part of the reason for writing about them was because I *wanted* to identify with them. I wanted to assimilate with Iranianness and to assimilate with Englishness. And then wanting not to assimilate, to *dis*-similate. And, of course, both have consequences.

Talking of consequences, after bringing out your wonderful pamphlet, Eve, are you working towards a full collection? Can you tell me something about it, without breaking the spell?

EED That's kind of you to ask. Currently I'm working on a collection of prose-ish lyric poems. It involves the idea of white passing, and whiteness as a feminising trait in relation to the female form. Various figures who represent the apex of feminine whiteness feature, from Virginia Woolf to Hayley Bieber to Catholic depictions of the angelic. I get the sense this collection is the beginning of a future ambition for my writing. I want to keep leaning into the complication of race, and in doing so, circumvent the expectation to prioritise proof or 'evidence' of the POC self, before valuing the lyric as an act of poetic craft. In other words, I want to treat my poems as something more expansive than just simply signifying a 'non-white' experience, despite how this can be marketable. Is there something you are currently working on?

MK Well, for my sins, I shall soon be working on putting a *Collected Poems* together for 2024. But I don't want to think about that just yet, as it will also be a 'big birthday' for me next year. For now, it's been such a pleasure to meet you, Eve, to hear your thoughts about poetry, and I wish you all the very best for what I hope will be a very long and playful journey for you in the future.

NINA MINGYA POWLES

SLIPSTITCH

can memory be unhoused or is it the form in which everything is held?
    – Victoria Chang, *Dear Memory*

humidity

My mother won't look inside her old piano.   The keys have
softened   and won't play.   She thinks something
might be growing inside,   the wood now warped
and damp.   Everything is porous   here.
My old memories are full   of holes. New ones   float
up to the surface,   sticky and   ready to be shaped.
I can hear the cousins' chatter about   heat lamps,
humidity, the local piano man.   I step into the
path of the electric fan   and part of my body becomes
air.   There are boxes of her records around my
feet, booklets   of sheet music with frayed corners
where she turned the pages   again and again.

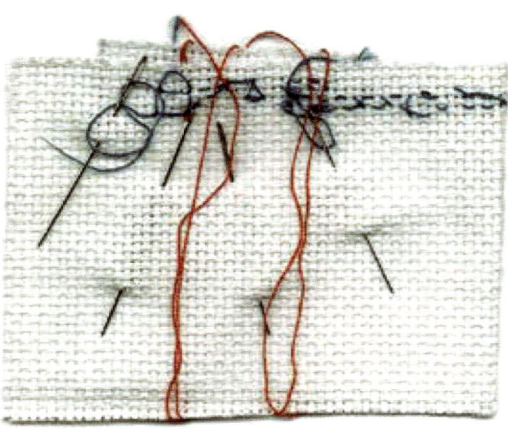

compartment

Next to the piano is the sewing machine, a black compact object set into its own wooden desk, the English words MADE IN THE PEOPLE'S REPUBLIC OF CHINA painted in gold on the side.

It's here that my grandfather stitched the quilts. He made four or five brightly coloured quilts in a short space of time, all in the early 1990s, all pieced together from fabric scraps and old garments belonging to my mother, her younger siblings, and my grandmother.

I had never noticed the sewing machine, yet it's pivotal to our favourite story about Gong Gong. Mum remembers once when the machine was stuck and wouldn't run. Gong Gong found a snake curled up inside the wooden treadle compartment. He pulled it out (here the details become blurry) and took it into the garden and shot it with his rifle.

work

Who does the machine belong to? Everyone remembers her using it, & also her trying to teach mum & my auntie how to sew with it & then much later he (a retired biologist) used it to begin his next piece of work when us cousins were born, which was a surprise to me when I found out the quilts were not made by her; & I was ashamed because of course I associate quilting & sewing with the work of women's hands, especially older women in the domestic space, & I struggled to picture him cutting out the small squares, pressing them & pinning them together in neat rows & slipstitching the brushed cotton binding by hand: his hand.

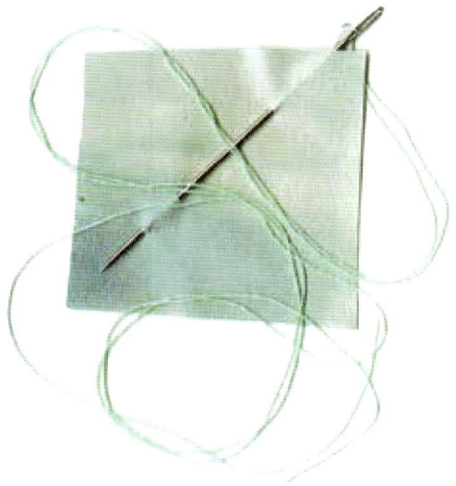

fragment

The machine belongs to memory and to a different time.

The machine belongs to the house, which still exists and also doesn't exist.

patchwork

His quilts are chaotic and lovely, composed of squares cut from old t-shirts and pyjamas and curtains and sarongs. The backing is a bright teal flannelette which has softened and become threadbare over time. Mum remembers the garments the squares were cut from. In each quilt block she sees a bright morning, a piano recital, a family trip to Taiwan in monsoon season.

patterning

A 'Germination' is a poetic form invented by Natalie Linh Bolderston, where each stanza can be read from left to right as well as from top to bottom within each triangle.

light	quilts	in
warmer countries	can keep	cool rain
in open windows	a pattern held	of threaded air

— — —

new	brittle	island
home of curving	river seams	coming loose
ocean light	the waves stitched	in slow hands

— — —

press	and	fold
the edge	by hand	with care
into the sea	pulled towards winter	from far away

— — —

backstitch

When I hold the quilt, the many pieces stitch themselves back together in the air.

A sleeve, a hidden pocket, a hand-stitched hem.

Threads crossing over the fold. A fragmentation in reverse.

The cut pieces can always be reused, but the threads remain.

handiwork

People asked me where I learned
and I said I taught myself the slow work of making.

But memory is a house with scraped white walls.
I step inside and choose what to take, what to leave behind.

My hands feel their way through
the gathering, the careful pulling apart.

cut

I cut out the pieces on the floor,   my knees pressed
against the scratched   floorboards. Two trees, a
wave,   a sun, a volcano, a buttery cloud. I lay
the   shapes   across   each   other   and   move   them,
testing   different   patterns   and   arrangements.   I
bend   down   and   crouch   over   them.   A   wave   touches
the   edge   of   the   slope.   A   cloud   passes   over   the
sun. Each scrap holding the outline   of another
garment,   another   self.   Another   home,
another   form. I cut and reshape them   in   my   hands,
pinning   to   keep   them   in   place. Time   moves
through   the   room,   leaves me in my quiet.

Essay

MAGIC PAPERS

On poetry pamphlets

Jeremy Noel-Tod

> Most conjuring shops and publishers were led by one person, each with very different priorities, budgets and tastes: an individualist bent which goes some way to accounting for the diversity of styles found across publications [...] It's important to remember that, during this period, there were hundreds of independent printers across the UK alone, adding another level of variation to the books and magazines produced. All of these factors combined to make the designs found in magic literature diverse, often unusual and sometimes bizarre.
> – Philip David Treece, *Magic Papers* (2020)

Change a few words of this quotation from a catalogue of twentieth-century 'conjuring ephemera', and you would have a working description of small-press poetry publishing. Both are modern subcultures that have thrived on a DIY ethic and individualist aesthetic, circulated among small readerships willing to buy on the strength of a name, a title, or even a fine cover. The more unusual and ephemeral such publications appear, the more attractive they become to the seeker of new tricks – which is why, in particular, I love poetry pamphlets.

I once ran a pamphlet press – called, with a sort of sincere irony, Landfill. I had previously worked the nightshift at *Anglia AutoTrader* magazine, captioning thumbnails of cars, so had a basic knowledge of the pirated publishing software I acquired. But otherwise, I didn't know much about book design. The simple A6 template I adopted came from talking with a local printer about how to produce single poetic sequences as a clean, tough, thin and cheap fold of paper. What people liked about these plain little books, when they saw and held them, was that they *were* little; appealing both to eye and hand. I'm lucky enough to be able to quote someone else's appreciative description: 'Staples and bright white wove, meringuey and crisped to the corners, fat bonny 12-point text bang in the middle of the page like visits to the newsagent to buy this term's new A4 and multi-coloured divider' (Christina McLeish).

I like this association of poetry with the excitement of new stationery. Each Landfill pamphlet was intended to feel like its own completed notebook; in the case of the title McLeish is describing, R.F. Langley's *Twine* (2004), each page held one nineteen-line stanza. The print runs weren't so limited as to be vanishingly exclusive: a couple of hundred each time. But the littleness, I think, created a sense of intimacy, as though you had been given a handwritten copy, as in the days of Shakespeare circulating (to quote a contemporary) 'his sugared sonnets among his private friends'.

Sugared sonnets make for social networks: the circulation of most pamphlets is by nature a personal business. Chain bookshops rarely stock publications lacking a legible spine, and similarly find the profit margin on the average pamphlet hard to see (that alternative term, 'chapbook', is etymologically related to 'cheap'). So the majority are sold direct, either at readings or by post. Online baskets have made this more anonymous than it used to be: Paypal, despite its name, does not require you to be pals. Neither did pre-digital commerce – but when I think of buying poetry by cheque, what I remember is writing out small sums longhand and paperclipping the signed sheet to a scribbled friendly note requesting the goods.

Those sums of pounds and pence were usually, of course, barely enough to cover printing and postage, let alone profit – the financial reality of pamphlet publishing is that it is close to a gift economy. This was the term Tim Atkins used when, at a reading where I had no cash, he generously gave me a copy of some of his versions of Petrarch, hand-printed in coloured inks by Crater Press on a single folded sheet that you had to slit with a knife. I hope I partly repaid the gift in spirit at least when I later typeset another sonnet from the sequence to distribute as a free broadside at a different reading. It ran:

> This
> poetry
> which is
> written
> to effect
> change
> in the world
> Usually printed in
> editions of
> less than
> 1000
> & read
> Only by poets
> O how I love it

The quiet love that's folded into the making of pamphlets can make the 'full collection' seem a cold fish as it swims into the Amazon warehouses and – if it's lucky – onto annual shortlists such as the T.S. Eliot Prize, which defines 'a "book" [...] as having at least 48 pages'. As J.T. Welsch's 2020 study of market forces in contemporary poetry argues, the spine-filling thickness of the modern poetry collection has emerged as the 'standardised currency of an increasingly institutionalised field' rather than a form with its own conceptual integrity (such as, say, the novel).

The problem with this artificial standardisation of what 'counts' in poetry culture can be illustrated by the case of Eliot himself, who is best known for sequences – such as *Prufrock and Other Observations* (1917) and *Ash-Wednesday* (1930) – which, in their first printings, would have fallen foul of the numerical rule now attached to his name (as would *The Waste Land* if it had not been plumped up with Notes). Eliot's strategy, he said in a letter, was to remember that each new publication 'should be an event' – and the streamlined realisation of them on the small-press model helped to make this happen.

When the Second World War broke out, Eliot's vision of the poem as an ink-and-paper event inspired what would eventually become three-quarters of *Four Quartets* (1943): a set of 'patriotic poems' written under and about the conditions of wartime life. Unbind the sequence, and it breaks down into a trio of pamphlets, published in the first three years of the war: *East Coker* (1940), *The Dry Salvages* (1941) and *Little Gidding* (1942). These proved so popular that *Burnt Norton* (1936), the first 'Quartet', was also reissued as a pamphlet, having first appeared in *Collected Poems 1909–1935* – a rare example of a poem in a book heading backwards into pamphlethood. It is also an unusual instance of the pamphlet signifying the high, rather than low, status of the author: Faber & Faber (where Eliot was poetry editor) was only able to obtain government license for this lavish use of rationed paper because of his commanding reputation as a poet and critic. To read *The Dry Salvages* in its first printing on rough, jaggedly cut rag paper, stapled in a simple card cover, is to feel what it calls, in its closing lines, 'distress of nations and perplexity'.

The political power of the pamphlet form becomes apparent when it changes the names you find on the poetry shelves. This century, that's exactly what the 'mouthmark' series from flipped eye publishing did in the UK. Established by Nii Ayikwei Parkes with the aim of getting 'poets from non-mainstream backgrounds – including performance – into print', and with a budget of only £300 per 'brown paper and black ink' title, it published first, less-than-full collections by, among others, Inua Ellams and Warsan Shire. The latter, famously, was quoted by Beyoncé on her visual album *Lemonade* (2016) – the release of which saw Shire's *Teaching My Mother How To Give Birth* (2011) leap from weekly sales of 78 to 764, and eventually (thanks to print-on-demand distribution) tens of thousands. But Ellams' *Thirteen Fairy Negro Tales* (2005) has also sold over 2,000 copies. That's a figure many poetry publishers would settle for, including Faber & Faber, whose *New Poets* series, launched with Arts Council funding in 2009, flipped eye can rightly claim to have inspired – although in Faber's case the initiative continued the firm's tradition of an almost entirely white poetry list (Zaffar Kunial being the one exception in sixteen pamphlets).

As both Parkes and Eliot knew, one of the superpowers of the pamphlet series with a clear purpose in the world is its appeal to an audience willing to extend its range. Cheap and portable, it can be bought in multiples, easily packed and posted everywhere (the poet Donald Davie remembered reading the wartime *Quartets* while in Arctic Russia with the Navy; somehow Warsan Shire got into Beyoncé's hands). At the same time, even when selling thousands, the spirit of the pamphlet is one of artistic intensity. Economy of pages implicitly requests your undivided attention. 'If you don't get it you're not listening', warned the mouthmark title page; 'you are the music / While the music lasts', Eliot told readers on the last page of *The Dry Salvages*.

When the perfect-bound collection undoes the stitching of the pamphlet it strips back an art object that at its most inventive extends the poetics of a text to typeface, graphics, shape, and paper stock. In a new collection of writings on *The Small Press Model* (Uniform Books), poet, artist, printer and publisher Simon Cutts beautifully describes the physical precision of such considerations as 'the flapability of the pamphlet':

> You can always tell the rightness of purpose of a pamphlet, the way it controls the draught between its pages, like an instrument, using the air generated as it is waved. It is its own mechanism, held together as a gathering of sheets, a relationship between the lightness of weight of the interior and a slightly heavier cover holding the folded pages. [...] The reader is calmed by its measure, its judgement of the weight of turning, and a symmetry of content revealed

Cutts' conceit of the pamphlet as a little breeze-machine took me back, happily, to my copy of Harry Gilonis's *Nine* (2022): a landscape booklet of nine classical haiku, in Japanese and English, published by Essence Press. Printed in pale grey ink on the slightly translucent paper used for traditional ink wash painting, the words shadow each other through the pages in a way that continues their recurring image of 'mist'. The whole thing is tied by a single, grasshopper-green thread. Reading it is like opening a small window onto a meadow.

Cutts' elaboration of his image of controlled air into the idea of the pamphlet as a kind of 'instrument' for its own recital is suggestive. It makes me think, with pleasure, of collaborating with Anthony Vahni Capildeo on their Landfill title, *Person Animal Figure* (2005). The three distinct voices of this prose sequence were represented by a roman, a sans serif, and a bold font, and fitted as far as possible onto pages that foregrounded the paragraph as a compositional unit, balancing the intensity of the sentences with a rhythm of pause and reflection. The penultimate section, which introduces the 'Figure', interrupted this rhythm with a suspension of the prose continuum: a page spread of centre-justified sentences describing what their writing figured in ink:

it leads as it beckons, beckons as
it mirrors, contracting, decontracting, by a
plumage spray of lines.

To be made aware of the perceptual act of reading itself at this moment is breathtaking.

This is not to insist, preciously, on the small-press pamphlet as the one true way to appreciate a poem. I first encountered *Person Animal Figure* as a performed text, when it moved me as sound; subsequently, it was reprinted with alternative typesetting in Capildeo's second book, *Undraining Sea* (2009), where it reached more readers. But neither is the painstaking small-press pamphlet simply a collector's item, to be kept in cellophane. I would value it in other ways: as the wrapping of a new piece of writing in a new experience of reading; as a memento of the human scale that is the starting point of any art we may later invest with greatness, immortality, etc; and as a material trace of the world that produced it. As the *Times Literary Supplement* noted of the latest shortlists for the Michael Marks Awards for Poetry Pamphlets, there is a trend now towards using paper and card recycled from sources such as brewer's grain and disposable coffee cups. To quote Philip David Treece's *Magic Papers: Conjuring Ephemera 1890–1960* again: 'the story of these magic papers is a tale of human ingenuity: working sometimes for commercial gain, but always for the love of magic'.

A SORT OF NET

Maggie Millner, Couplets: A Love Story, *Faber, £12.99,*
ISBN 9780571376711
Sarala Estruch, After All We Have Travelled, *Nine Arches Press,*
£10.99, ISBN 9781913437527
Lavinia Singer, Artifice, *Prototype, £12,* ISBN 9781913513351

Clare Pollard on three artful debuts

. . .

Robert Frost famously once declared that writing free verse is like playing tennis with the net down. These three debut collections are very different, but if there is a link between them it would be that they all want to play with the net 'up' – they have a particular concern with the relationship between form and content, which makes it possible to see their technique and subject matter evolving symbiotically across their pages.

Perhaps this is most obvious in Maggie Millner's *Couplets*, a verse-novel about the speaker leaving a long-term boyfriend to begin a passionate affair with a woman – uncoupling and coupling – written largely in rhymed couplets, although occasionally interspersed with prose poems. Rhyme itself, same but different, becomes a metaphor within these pages for sexual attraction – rhyme is, after all, about anticipation, reflection and otherness. The 'Proem' which begins the collection sets out these themes with stunning clarity:

> My eye loved

everything it fell upon.
    And then one day it fell upon

a mirror. And he was nowhere
    in the mirror. And she was everywhere.

Millner writes the way that she claims to have had sex in adolescence: 'with a rabid, abstract interest / in experience', and the poems are crammed with very specific details – vapes, a Rachel Cusk quote, natural wine, ferns, Ottolenghi cake, the particleboard and 'wooden dowels' of furniture – as well as very intimate detail, from a sexual fantasy involving owl-masks to her girlfriend's bag of lubricants. However, the prosy rhythms and erudite, slant rhymes create an atmosphere, simultaneously, of flatness and distance. The effect is very similar to that of Hannah Sullivan's poetry – I was reminded on many occasions of 'You, Very Young in New York' from her T.S. Eliot Award-winning *Three Poems*. Millner's poem about being constrained, both sexy and bathetic (Everyone had the same Ikea bed. / She tied my wrists to hers, above my head.') acts as a kind of *Ars Poetica*. Another Millner poem, reproduced in full here, further demonstrates the technique:

> When I was with her, the physical
>   experience of my pleasure – *the little*
>
> *death* – seemed to make the nauseous question
>   of whether I was in possession
>
> of a clear and unified self
>   mostly irrelevant. Those days, I was something else:
>
> a soft vacuity. A sort of net.
>   No guilt, no age. No epithet.
>   ('1.7')

A later poem also highlights the philosophical intent of the sequence. For all this is a delicious, dirty and deadpan account of a love affair, its most central question is: who am I?

> Now and then, I'd get the strange impression
> that she was me. A stab of chthonic recognition

If you enjoy the word 'chthonic' as much as I do there, then this is a book for you.

After All We Have Travelled by Sarala Estruch is a collection about family: daughterhood and motherhood. It is also about language(s) and silence(s), and as such is most interesting where Estruch is playing with form. Her natural unit often seems to be a very short line, but rather than filling the book with long, skinny poems, lineation is marked by an oblique – the lines all shoving and jostling up against each other – or poems are made up of two columns, allowing for different readings and connections across or down. The poems themselves, then, seem to visually gesture at intimacies and distances, as in 'Aerogramme (II)':

Blue envelope careens	through the letterbox –
dutiful dove, wrong-	hued, fluttering to
the *Welcome* mat	A letter folded
into itself	like a weeping child

'Turtle' works particularly well, with its dance between closeness and the fear of it (or fear of its retreat):

a body rushes forward	to embrace another
in a curl of saline froth	& desire
then retreats –	always
there is the retreat	–

Elsewhere, in poems such as 'I love everything about being a mother' gaps are used to suggest the fragmented mind of the sleep-deprived parent, whose self now seems made up of absences and lucid moments, whose face is:

linen   stre t ch ed o v er   the rack
of me   blustering   in a careless wind

The playful and moving 'Camera Lucida' is a meditation on a lost father laid out like a photograph album, with short poems in the spaces where photos should be. The poet uses empty pages to powerful effect, whilst an image of a rose – that 'red disaster' on a stalk – leads to the revelation:

The photograph stuns me

I am looking at [a rose through the] *eyes* [of my father]

– the closest I have been to him in decades

'Bouchon' is a witty meditation of the collection's themes, in which the speaker notes her first word, in her first language (French), means 'bottleneck', leading to the thought that language itself can be a kind of stopper that 'holds things down', whereas:

> ... in the land
> of my father and my father's father, I know
> so little my hungry mind gorges, fed to
> bursting. There are no stoppers –

This is an intelligent book, provocative and pulsing with its stop-start rhythms.

Lavinia Singer's collection, *Artifice*, is explicitly about craft: its authenticity and artificiality. While it perhaps lacks the immediacy and intimacy of the other collections, it provides a different sort of pleasure in its finely wrought objets d'art. There are many concrete poems in the collection, mimicking boxes, waxworks, a compass rose, a bookworm (that could also be a book's spine) and Hildegard von Bingen's vision of 'The Cosmic Egg'. The poem 'ATLAS' is shaped as a pyramid, and also an A, with the letter A running up each side. Poems are printed sideways; Singer makes ludic use of white space, notes and erasures.

The excellent 'The Painting of the Queen' after a Tudor portrait of Queen Elizabeth I by an unknown English artist contrasts an account of the beauty routines of the time with the language of art restoration, to suggest that – though we may now live in an age of filters – portraits have always involved fantasy and falsification:

> *For cleansing the Skin, anoint with*
> *the oyl of sweet Almonds*
>   Applied varnish
>   and a thermoplastic resin
> *The Venetian Ceruse whitens*
> *with shine like a Pearl*
>   Characteristic blanching
>   and thick chalking across all
> *But for stubbournest Markes*
> *employ black patches cut in Starres or half Moons*

> The most damaged parts
> are coated in opaque over-paint

Keats's 'Ode on a Grecian Urn' haunts this book – in its thinginess and artistry – and in particular the lines: 'Beauty is truth, truth beauty, – that is all / Ye know on earth, and all ye need to know'. Singer's own 'True Artifice' seems determined to unpick this, daring to contradict what is too often taken as a truism:

> Beauty is difficult, unlike the telling of beautiful untrue things,
> things that don't exist: a good island, mystery's holy guardian,
> garden of bright images, our perfection, man-made dream,
> dreams like a diadem. For a few bright moments to be reborn,
> resolutely artificial, enigmatical, through art. To what end?
> End up as a book or work – neither begins nor ends; pretend.

I caught here a suggestion, too, of Yeats's 'Sailing to Byzantium', where the artist is transfigured into that wholly unnatural bird of 'hammered gold' that sings 'Of what is past, or passing, or to come', only to realise – when reading the footnotes – that the poem is that fiendish contraption, a Cento sonnet, and uses a line from that poem (also quoting, among others, Huysmans, Mallarmé and Wilde).

This feels a slightly unfashionable book – learned, riddling, serious and almost grand – but as such it is also quite unlike any other debut I have read in recent years. I was deeply impressed by its breadth and ambition, as well as the commitment – shared with Millner and Estruch – to keep playing with poetic constraint in new and risky ways.

Clare Pollard was born in Bolton in 1978. She has published five collections of poetry with Bloodaxe, the latest of which is Incarnation *(2017).*

WHAT WILL I DO IN THE FUTURE?

Hannah Sullivan, Was It for This, *Faber, £12.99*
ISBN 9780571362271
Solmaz Sharif, Customs, *Bloomsbury, £9.99,* ISBN 9781526655295
Will Harris, Brother Poem, *Granta, £10.99,* ISBN 9781915051042

Vidyan Ravinthiran on dissensus, within and between and beyond books of poems

. . .

I'm grateful to these books – works operating as wholes, crisscrossed by subtle (and sometimes sledgehammer) recurrences – for helping me think through what required thinking through, at a difficult time. We should all read widely in those different to us: but it would be remiss not to observe, in these collections, concerns also mine – such things as, turning the page, leap out almost violently (as if the writer read your mind). Communicational struggles, checkpoints, gatekeeping. Migration, and minoritisation within centres of power ('Downwind', writes Solmaz Sharif – an intriguing choice of word – 'I walked the wide hallways / of a great endowment'). Intergenerational suffering. Being rescued, in the doldrums of pandemic parenting, by Peppa Pig. A simultaneous dependence on, and suspicion of, the trope of trauma – that's too plotted, and is to be countered by a redeeming near-randomness of mental noise, manifesting creatively before lapsing toward the usual parameters. A yearning for a poetics not of identity (though none of the voices in these collections denies its coordinates) but of relation. With, attached to it, the idea that if and when we don't find the people we need (to be close to), we have a way of inventing them.

*

Hannah Sullivan writes about property (at contrastive points in her book she appears as a tenant, a homeowner and an estate agent) and about being mistaken for someone or something that you're not (when it's assumed you're deaf, but really you have a speech impediment and a foreign accent). Like Wordsworth, from whose *Prelude* she borrows her title (also, like memoirists whose autofiction might be seen as continuing Wordsworth's project) she writes about encounters with other people. This means risking accusations of voyeurism and – speaking of property, and how some increasingly consider lived experiences as possessions – of appropriation. In 'Tenants', she evokes the Grenfell fire in the spirit of Joseph Conrad, for whom the writer's task is 'by the power of the written word to make you hear, to make you feel – it is, before all, to make you see.' If we're to get beyond officialese – 'this report is avowedly provisional. / We wait further evidentiary material' – and really feel for others, it would seem necessary:

> To see the length and breadth and depth of hell.
>
> [...]
>
> To hear the short cough petulant the hosepipe made, being
>   trodden on,
> Staccato of the skull against the stairs, the water jets,
> The slop of firemen wrestling the carcass down

There's something uneasy about this. 'Short cough petulant' is incongruously Miltonic (the two adjectives, sandwiching a noun). What is the relation between style (Sullivan also works variations on Wordsworth's pentameter) and the guilt of the outsider-observer? Turning to Solmaz Sharif, and 'Dear Aleph':

> Empathy means
>
> laying yourself down
> in someone else's chalklines
>
> and snapping a photo.

*

I am also grateful to be asked, as someone with doubts about the group review, to – after a considerable hiatus, that has seen my life alter considerably – write such a review: a chance to explore those doubts. (As Adam Phillips might add: only our doubts are ever worth exploring.) I don't mean to reduce Sharif's poem to a contradiction of Sullivan's; but the danger of such reviews is typically the opposite, of generating false consensus. Diversity is given lip-service then swiftly annulled. How might we present poetic works as, instead, in (sometimes frictive) conversation? Will Harris lists some of his sources for *Brother Poem* but leaves others to be discovered. Poetic allusion is conversation by other means, and these echoes are, often, of verse in which people talk: Matthew Arnold's 'Dover Beach' ('what is / known might be as one / withdrawing at the other's / roar'), or the spalled confab of Saturn and Thea in Keats's *Hyperion*: 'where / the dead leaf fell there / did it rest and the tree / being one leaf less / words filled the gap'. The central conceit of *Brother Poem* – its address to a sibling who never existed – is a way of being one step ahead, concerning hot-topic issues of uniqueness and shareability. But it is not only that:

> What will I do
> in the future
>
> Use I or him
> when I mean you

A range of tones: curiosity, desperation, impatience – a question is asked and (possibly) self-answered, although the absent question mark prevents it from becoming wholly, acidly, rhetorical. When this poet is topical (mentioning, say, masks and isolation) it is in conscientious shorthand: his real allegiance is to the unobvious. But he tries for a humane route, towards those moments of illuminating surprise. Harris is – though his own style makes one suspicious of phrasemaking, of too-insistent declarations – my generation's W.H. Auden.

*

From Sharif's 'The Master's House':

> To date briefly a banker, a lapsed Marxist, and hear him on the
> phone speaking in billions of dollars, its residue over the

clear bulbs of his eyes, as he turns to look upon your nudity
To fantasise publishing a poem in the *New Yorker* eviscerating
    his little need

How little our clapbacks and subtweets amount to, in the end. (Appropriation is more complex than it may seem: we appropriate others – even if we leave them unnamed – to the stories we tell about ourselves.) These are the new master's tools and as such – to return to Audre Lorde, and the quotation providing this poem with its title – will never dismantle his house.

Sharif's work shapes me. The extremities of her language constitute a high-wire act that for many of us – as both persons and poets – has become indispensable. Edward Said applied the shattering of verb tenses, of the Victorian poet Gerard Manley Hopkins, to the Palestinian deprived of their history and reduced to a 'lonely began'. In 'The End of Exile', Sharif returns to Iran but (like one of Harris's personae, 'in Beijing expecting / the thud of recognition') can't restore the original loss: 'A without which / I have learned to be.' Eadweard Muybridge, she notices, proved that, while galloping, 'horses fly a moment'. Four pages later, she revisits the idea:

    The

    glass appears in hundreds
    of frames before reaching
    the prisoner's lips. In
    between each frame, the grief

    our eyes jump to create
    movement

The stanza break is virtuosic. Everything we see – including our visions of victims and aggressors, prisoners and gaolers – is mentally recreated, half-created and half-perceived. How much unwanted immortality has been conferred on people with no choice in the matter, by the power of screens?

Appropriation is more complex than we think.

*

Disordered finances and disordered time. Moving uneasily between the UK and the US, Sullivan 'towards the end of the heatwave' – in July 2020 – drives 'to Oldfield Circus in Northolt, where my life had begun'. Prose mingles with lineated verse; an, I think, echo – 'It was all bland, harmonious, / and given to us: / a ravishing for-nothingness' – of the end of Elizabeth Bishop's 'Poem'. (Bishop called herself a 'minor female Wordsworth', a more subversive than self-deprecating statement.) Sullivan returns to her old street:

> 'Lived round here long?' I asked, unable to think of anything better. It was a cold, sharp March morning and my sinuses hurt. In the gutter a pigeon was exploring a long strip of orange peel, flattened to a map.

> The woman outside number 39, on the other side of the road, was doing something complicated with two bins. I made a flaccid gesture of offering to help – knowing that the full-hearted version of the gesture would now seem a threat.

The prose rhymes: 'better' and 'gutter'. Making-sense-of-things turns, with that downbeat, to fatalism, a helplessness only mildly alleviated by the creative transformation of orange peel into a – the writer-observer, scanning her environment, finds a shred of meaning – symbolic map. (Even the number 39 may be important, in this book about being a woman entering her forties.) The poet too is 'doing something complicated', in a polarised society where one cannot reach those 'on the other side' without – it can feel – being wilfully and wailfully misunderstood.

Another prose rhyme: *knowing* leads to and firms up, accentuates, 'now', a word with multiple meanings. 'Now', as in, Sullivan, or her speaker, has 'now' hovered too long hasn't raced to help, and to do so at this point – too late – would seem at the best obtuse and at the worst patronising, even accusatory. But 'now' also means: at this point in time – when people with much in common struggle to converse, and our politics of suspicion descends, frequently, into paranoia.

I was heartened recently by these words from Jon Stone: 'We could learn to respond to our anxiety and fragility by attending much more assiduously to all those neglected, minor opportunities to better know one another [...] It means building fine, complex networks of mutual understanding and tentative trust.' The pulses of life begin to beat again. I'm thinking of Charles Lamb when he was thinking about *Macbeth*; since I don't know how to parse the power of Sharif's lines, which are about, I suspect, the work of disentangling the experience of being known, from the feeling of being threatened:

Would you have knocked for me?
I ask the neighbor.

I have been, he said.

Then I felt his knocking

        ]]

inside my chest.

Vidyan Ravinthiran has written two collections of poetry. His latest books are Worlds Woven Together, *a collection of his essays on verse, and* Spontaneity and Form in Modern Prose.

ORGANISATIONAL STRUCTURES

Joe Carrick-Varty, More Sky, *Carcanet*, £11.99,
ISBN 9781800173019
Akwaeke Emezi, Content Warning: Everything, *Bloomsbury*, £12.99,
ISBN 9781526658678
Degna Stone, Proof of Life on Earth, *Nine Arches*, £10.99,
ISBN 9781913437589

Alycia Pirmohamed on the shaping of three new collections

. . .

Natasha Sajé writes that 'many times when readers open a book, they don't read the poems in the order they have been arranged'. She goes on to ask: does it matter, then, how a collection of poems is organised?

It does matter, though perhaps how much it matters depends on the book. What fascinates me about all three of these debuts – Joe Carrick-Varty's *More Sky*; Degna Stone's *Proof of Life on Earth*; and Akwaeke Emezi's *Content Warning: Everything* – comes down to structure, and I think reading each in sequence pulls forward deeper and more interesting narratives than would come through otherwise. Sajé calls a collection's organisation its 'gesture', referring to how a book 'carries itself to a reader', and in these collections, this kind of gesturing is intentional and intelligently achieved. While sequencing a collection is generally a thoughtful process for most authors, I'd argue that the patterning feels especially coherent in these three books.

This is possibly because, to varying degrees, these collections fall under the category of a poetry 'project book'. Cynthia Marie Hoffman writes: '[a] poetry project book is easily identified by its often strikingly singular focus or its relentless adherence to a formal constraint'. *More Sky* is the best example of this. Carrick-Varty's poems orbit obsessively around the subject of suicide, particularly in relation to the speaker's father but also in relation to the self. The description of the poems as obsessive isn't a thematic judgement; it is an acknowledgement of Carrick-Varty's deliberate craft, such as how the words 'suicide' and 'dad' fissure syntax or build toward a peculiar, intriguing, kind of grammar; how an obsessive pacing is constructed through formal elements; how poems move discursively in response to themes of literal and metaphorical loss.

This last technique is especially impressive in *More Sky*. Carrick-Varty's poetry resists linearity and predicated composition, which feels true to how one might experience trauma. Poetic resonances don't, and in fact can't, drive these poems, or if they do, they are made external to the speaker:

Once upon a time when suicide was a storm that stripped
  comparison from the landscape
  a therapist once likened my sadness
  to a tree's collection of year rings.
                                                    ('sky doc')

These discursive movements lead to surprising and exciting imagistic formations, and for me, the constant pressure on imagery is crucial to the success of this book. In *More Sky,* we begin to expect the subject matter early on, as each poem imagines or reflects on suicide and/or a father's alcoholism, and so meaning is enhanced instead by how gaps appear or disappear, how our expectations are subverted. I am reminded of Diana Khoi Nguyen's *Ghost Of,* where visible gaps and breaks in language are integral to the poetry. Carrick-Varty's holes and ruptures are more metaphorically persistent than Nguyen's corporal cut-outs, but the impact is similar – an inability to articulate an experience unless it illustrates, also, how loss changes perspective. For example, the sequence 'From the Perspective of Coral' replaces expected vocabulary with the word 'suicide':

There are a large number of particulates suspended
in the ocean, and while suicide does not
have eyelashes to keep particulates out of its eyes
as humans do, it emits a certain frequency
(some call it a hum, a toothache,
the background wind of a 4am voicemail)

There is the danger that the subject matter and rhetorical strategy of disruption become somewhat predictable. The manipulation of language in the long poem 'sky doc' which takes up the full second half of the collection, begins to feel less surprising over time. Even still, many of my favourite moments are in this half, which remains effective despite this.

Content Warning: Everything is the debut book of poems by Akwaeke Emezi, a well-renowned fiction writer. Emezi's background as a novelist is perhaps why this book also feels so deliberately organised. It reads almost chronologically, the narrative driven by both an overarching story and the characterisation of recurring figures throughout. While it traverses multiple themes within a variety of literal and mythical places, and it isn't as singularly focused as a 'project book', Emezi's consistent formal and stylistic choices create greater cohesion.

In her essay, Sajé quotes Neil Fraistat's definition of 'contexture': 'the contextuality provided for each poem by the larger frame within which it is placed, the intertextuality among poems so placed, and the resultant texture of resonance and meanings.' Emezi is particularly skilful at placing poems next to one another, often complicating a poem's meaning by its proximity to another piece. For example, the two poems 'Healing' and 'I Thought I Could Be Well' are side-by-side, and this sequence enhances the emotional intricacy of both. 'Healing' ends with an assertion of safety:

the kitten curls up against my arm / i remind myself i am safe now

we fall asleep / in the line of the afternoon sun

Yet on the next page, 'I Thought I Could Be Well' begins with the word 'still' as if the poem is a continuation of what came before: '*still*, how i hunger for hunger', Emezi writes. The diction becomes more agitated, subverting the peaceful end of 'Healing', and reminding readers that there is an inconstant and difficult journey toward recuperation and self-discovery.

Formally, there is an emphasis on prose poems. While these pieces are expansive in imagination – the speaker inserts themselves as a character in the Bible, whether as the sibling of Jesus, lover of Magdalene, or relative of Mary, making the book an enthralling, queered allegorical text – I feel they do tend to privilege storytelling elements like worldbuilding over other poetic strategies. While some readers will prefer this, I favour the other forms, where linebreaks and associative imagery propel the work forward, such as the striking 'Salvation':

> i believe in new skins, even nightmares
> can be maps, space between existence
> and function, between performance and effect
> if you are made of the skins of what you do
> how do you choose your supple hides
> with the sour guilt? the ecstatic evil?

There are also prose-like poems in this collection where Emezi varies their approach – pieces like 'Oh Delilah' or the remarkable title poem. Here the use of slashes or the lack of punctuation make the poems feel akin to what Carl Phillips, in *My Trade is Mystery*, distinguishes as not necessarily prose poems that have 'abandoned' linebreaks, but rather poems made up of single-line stanzas. Emezi has great control over these pieces and, though it is a slim volume, *Content Warning: Everything* is a powerful book.

Degna Stone's *Proof of Life on Earth* has a similarly cumulative effect. Stone weaves together figurative and literal notions of the heart: love, examined through romantic and familial relationships, and medical conditions of the bodily heart, the organ itself. Though in the book's last two thirds, this emphasis on the heart is less obvious, the atmosphere remains tender and is held together by this initial framework.

While Stone does not always use traditional forms themselves, she does incorporate many features of them. Lines carry a purposeful rhythm, both related to the musicality implicit to the diction and Stone's practice of refrains or other kinds of repetition. These echoes – coming back to contexture – are particularly exciting in *Proof of Life on Earth*, creating a layered reading of the book's many themes, some of which include love, the body, empire and resistance, and landscape and place.

The language in *Proof of Life on Earth* is often stripped back, which is a quality of Stone's voice and is generally successful. However, it can at times make the poetry feel aphoristic, like the closing lines of 'Vegan in

Pearls' or 'Ruby, Aged 4½' – both end on conclusive statements about life and death. But generally, the poems are specific and impactful. This is particularly true of longer pieces, where Stone extends a phrase or a thought for a moment longer and unearths unexpected connections. The sequence poem 'Vörður' is captivating for this reason and holds many pleasurable lines:

> The city shifts.
>> We find ourselves
>>> At the ghost of the old shoreline,
>
> where you tell me tales of houses that wander through town
> and statues that walk from overlooked corners to find a home
> where the swans protect us from nykur but not ourselves.

There are poems, too, where the aforementioned restraint in language is effective in how it matches restraint in form. The pantoum 'At Snook Tower' is a piece where language feels enclosed in an inescapable repetition yet still echoes with possibility:

> The sound of rainfall arrives inside your head,
> close your eyes; he begins to disappear.
>
> As jellyfish dry into patterns on sand,
> base notes of wood smoke play on the breeze.
> Close your eyes; he begins to disappear
> as timber markers wait to drown at high tide.

Throughout *Proof of Life on Earth,* Stone effectively translates how one experiences particular places. Toward the book's end, especially, the landscape is a thriving and important presence. With an oscillating ambivalence and rootedness in relation to place, there is a satisfying tension in the way Stone attends to how both heart and land hold memory.

Alycia Pirmohamed is a Canadian-born poet based in Scotland. She is the author of Another Way to Split Water.

EXCAVATING LANGUAGE

Briony Hughes, Rhizomes, *Broken Sleep, £16.99*
ISBN 9781915079626
James Wilkes, Mille Regretz, *Pamenar Press, £14*
ISBN 9781915341020
Colin Herd and Maria Sledmere, Cocoa and Nothing,
Spam Press, £12, ISBN 9781915049186

Astra Papachristodoulou on mourning, reverberations
and consolation

. . .

Maggie O'Sullivan has referred to writing poetry as a process of uncovering words and energies, an excavation of the soils of language. Briony Hughes' *Rhizomes*, a collection of poems written in response to the August 2020 Chobham Common fire in Surrey, is very much an echo of this idea. Supple in its range of registers and forms, the collection is divided into five distinctive sequences that all come together to paint a picture of a vulnerable and charred world. Quick-paced yet tender lines are often scattered across the landscape of the page, sometimes in diary form and sometimes disguised as footnotes, to enhance this element of brokenness. Observing and listening to what 'some of us watched unfold on the telly / others in the cities' means surrendering to yet engaging (to some degree) with the catastrophic effects of climate change.

Rhizomes opens with a series of fairly bold, despondent lyrics that seek to establish the urgent tone that runs throughout. The collection starts with the following lines: 'Everything was fucked and the silence and the loss or the day-to-day / had got me or all of us'. This initial 'us' adds a sense of plurality early on and asserts collective mourning – around broad themes such as climate change – as a response familiar to many readers.

The second sequence in the collection 'Rhizomes or Taproot' (below) is particularly effective and striking in its form, with stretching roots (or sometimes a lack of) informing the architecture of the poems visually. In contrast to the other sequences in the book, the poems in this section have been hand-stamped with black ink, an act that predisposes us to physical force and relates to the charred landscape evoked by Hughes – in the same way an inked stamp leaves a footprint when it comes in contact with the page, a wildfire leaves behind a landscape overwhelmed with charred remnants of burned vegetation and animals. This aesthetic choice not only communicates well with the overall theme of destruction which produces further meaning, but also enhances the intimate tone of the poems. Hughes' lyrics are swept away by the rapture of the fire; the concrete poems in this section become textual gestures with a kind of kinetic energy that pulses outward:

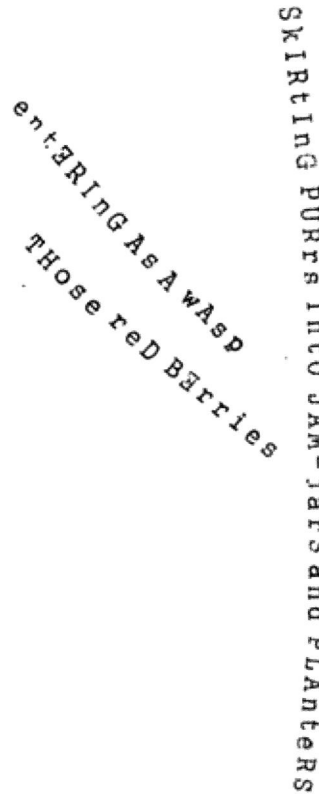

In this example, language is fragmented and adrift, like remnants of the fire that disturbed the once-unspoilt nature reserve. Death and downfall come together in this untitled poem, but so does hope. These take minimal but essential physical space on the page, the tree-shaped poem may be leafless and rootless but is *still standing*.

The collection's final line 'go beyond the one two one two one two to read and finally / take this with a pinch of each of us' didn't quite offer the closure that I sought as a reader, but perhaps this was intentional given the context of the book. Saying that, what stayed with me were the following lines, also from the final sequence, that open up a dialogue for the interconnectedness between humans and nonhumans in the Anthropocene: 'what is a body without organs / a kind of husk / or several husks or bodies'.

Like *Rhizomes*, James Wilkes's *Mille Regretz* also experiments with textual fragmentation and collaging in interesting ways. Beautifully made by Pamenar Press, *Mille Regretz* reimagines the chansons of the Renaissance composer Josquin des Prez, and weaves visual, verbal and sonic threads into a polyphonic macramé of language. The book's title takes its name from Josquin's homonymous chanson, a moderately slow and melancholic piece which narrates the pain of leaving one's beloved, 'A thousand regrets at deserting you and leaving behind your loving face' (from French: 'Mille regretz de vous abandoner / et d'eslonger vostre fache amoureuse').

As Wilkes notes in the book's afterword, the poems use Josquin's secular chansons, his printed scores and partial lyrics, as a starting point. Rather than offering direct translations, the poet borrows processes seen in Josquin's work as means of inspiration. Wilkes writes that 'his was a very procedural kind of music, and I found ways to repurpose – to translate – a number of these techniques'. I found Wilkes' afterword at the back of the book incredibly useful, especially given the conceptual form of the book.

This reflexive and sometimes haunting collection of poems asks us to meditate on the musicality of language through repetition and tonal resonance: 'Silk and stone. Silk over stone. See the bones of it. / Crisp edges'. The aural qualities of the words 'silk', 'stone' and 'bones' in combination with their elemental and material dimensions fuse in meditative multitude. This eerie dimension was enhanced when

I played Josquin des Prez's respective songs in the background while reading the poems – songs and poems fused in perfect harmony.

Another example along these lines comes from the poem 'Plaine de deuil' which is a poised excavation of the title's, and respective song's, reference to 'deuil', meaning 'mourning' in English:

> and now you're in the sea, not the sea of being like the real sea –
> saltwater in your ears, gulping it down, burns your throat and the
> green wave moves you up it like an escalator that intends to drown.

This is one of the numerous achingly moving moments of textual intensity in the book. In these lines, grief is steeped in a shared language, it becomes a kind of grief that is 'gulped down', hurting the body. The lack of coherence in some of the other poems can be challenging at times, however meaning is re-energised by noise and active listening to 'the clarity of its harmonics'.

Fizzing with bounding rhythms, *Mille Regretz* ends with 'Nymphes des bois' an enigmatic poem written in response to another Josquin des Prez song – a lament composed on the occasion of the death of his predecessor Johannes Ockeghem. The reader's journey ends with a bracing dive into contemplations of the temporal: 'Alive in an inkscape / broke with wishing / put your heart in a vitrine / the mountains leer'.

Maria Sledmere and Colin Herd's collaborative book *Cocoa and Nothing* is a Ritter Sport-themed collection that, much like its square-shaped chocolate muse, brings comfort with the turn of each page ('froth / like a poem / and a secret, / that old 90s / chocolate bar'). The content is multitudinous, as if a child had found the hidden tub of Quality Streets, then unwrapped and devoured every different flavour before they got caught. Playfully unapologetic, the book is powered by the thrill of living. The poems are sifted through the nostalgic and everyday – we encounter yearbooks, meal deals, oversized scrunchies and friendly Uber drivers.

Deceptively simple and cosy, yet nuanced in most places, in the poem 'Cornflakes', chocolate eating becomes a ritual: ''fabula' and 'syuzhet' / doesn't make sense when / you wake up and pour poetry / on cornflakes / it's so everyday / gorgeous disorder [...] I said pour it on your cornflakes / until you feel better'. Chocolate eating and poetry consumption appear to be vehicles of consolation for the poet who is 'living under the wrapper / inside which this poem / sleeps soundlessly / insulated after the storm'.

Throughout these poems there is a desire for escape – an accumulation of insatiable cravings ('eat the ecstasy seed' or 'I love you the most little spoon') and tension arising from the absence of punctuation and textual fragmentation throughout. For instance, in 'Cranberry Nuss', the speaker who 'has seen enough / round here to never / grow myself again' unfolds their thoughts in a continuous, non-linear way, as a means to enhance the poem's spontaneous and personal tone. This poem, beyond its fleeting references to Ocean Spray cranberry juice and berry-triggered trypophobia, ends with a despairing note – even chocolate is unable to alleviate the discomfort of the speaker:

> a real mouthful
> tastes better when the paranoia is over
> let's be free
> don't mind if you squash me

This is a dense pudding of a book. Sledmere and Herd's energy-packed poems are evidence of the expansive possibility of poetry, working in disparate contexts, forms and registers – this is enhanced by the collaborative effort of the poets who naturally bring different voices to the table, creating a chemistry that cannot be denied. *Cocoa and Nothing* ends with a long prose poem ('Dark Whole Hazelnuts') whose words unravel like a stream of consciousness in page form: 'I love my lung capacity and the pedal piano in the song 'All my Friends', some of them are allergic to all nuts – I'm scared of dark chocolate because it's just too much'. Like a bar of chocolate, *Cocoa and Nothing* sometimes surprises, but always satiates.

Astra Papachristodoulou's debut poetry collection Constellations *was released in 2022 with Guillemot Press.*

POETS WITH GUTS TO SPARE

Jen Calleja, Dust Sucker, *Makina, £8, ISBN 9781739616007*
Kandace Siobhan Walker, Kaleido, *Bad Betty, £10,*
ISBN 9781913268336
Kathryn Bevis, Flamingo, *Seren, £6, ISBN 9781781726938*
Ellora Sutton, Antonyms for Burial, *Fourteen Poems, £8,*
ISBN 9781838394363
Tim Tim Cheng, Tapping at Glass, *Verve Press, £7.99,*
ISBN 9781913917296

SZ Shao on a selection of recent poetry pamphlets

...

Having your work ghettoised as 'feminist' is an occupational hazard for female artists. We all know how it works. When a woman writes about her gendered experiences, she is writing about being female – whereas when a man writes about his gendered experiences, he is writing about being human. Reading these five pamphlets, all coincidentally written by poets using she/her pronouns, I was deeply struck by the unapologetically femme motifs such as motherhood, breasts, grandmas and flowers recurring across them all. It takes real creative guts to not compartmentalise being a girl and being an artist who wants to be taken seriously. Fortunately for us, these are poets with guts to spare.

Jen Calleja's *Dust Sucker* comes as close to time travel as poetry can. In this pamphlet-length poem, Calleja contends with an overwhelming sense of temporal instability, of slipping uncontrollably between past and future. The poet is never quite wearing the right thing, as if her body is out of sync with her life. She's a girl in a second-hand swimsuit, 'previous owner probably eighty'. Her shoes aren't right for this forest hike either. Now she's a woman squeezed into 'a musty latex catsuit from the eighties'. The sometimes dreamy imagery belies tightly coiled anxieties and a deep preoccupation with death. A mundane household noise 'foreshadows a gas explosion'. Childhood memories are tainted by jarringly adult fretting. It's like the present moment can't hold the author tightly enough. The speaker is 'a sand castle of a woman', and the poems here are equally unstable. It teeters on a knife edge, unsure how to approach things which will one day not be.

Calleja's hypervigilance and troubles with time will feel viscerally familiar to readers living with trauma, with its power to leave us stuck in those moments of overwhelming unsafeness, struggling to rejoin the forward flow of life. *Dust Sucker* is a quietly courageous, quietly devastating portrait of grief in motion. It deals specifically with the poet's loss of gendered time, as infertility forces her to find a way of structuring life beyond the cycles of motherhood. The poem is packed with fertility imagery, which weighs on the reader as they gradually come to understand the shape of the poet's bereavement. The poet must learn how to keep moving forwards, while understanding that dust is the future tense of every word, in every language: that life is a relentless process of conjugating backwards from death. By the end, Calleja has made an art form of becoming dust.

Ellora Sutton's hair-raisingly beautiful poetry is written with a wild strength of heart. In the opening poem of *Antonyms for Burial*, for example, the speaker describes herself in passing as having 'the heart of a fighting rooster'. Elsewhere the work is brimming with deep faith in enchantment and the transformative power of everything from songbirds to Haribo Starmix to queer love:

I use so much moisturiser it is almost like being touched.
[...]
I finish with oil, call myself *anointed*,
the day *blaring* and *mine*. Ceiling:

I am not a ceiling. I am a bird.

In my first reading of 'Diana, or The Huntress', which ends with the above lines, I pencilled in the margin, 'how can such surreal imagery feel so full of meaning?' Five or six readings in, and I'm still unsure how Sutton's magic operates. All I know is that until I read *Antonyms for Burial*, I had never really understood what people meant when they described something as 'arresting'. This is poetry that will truly stop you in your tracks. From the very first line, it raises you in its teeth by the scruff of your neck. Your feet will not touch the floor again for a very long time.

Kaleido by Kandace Siobhan Walker is a compelling showcase of human capacity. She notes, for example, 'A strength of our species is its ability to build churches / out of whatever washes up on the beach.' The disjointed flotsam and jetsam of her life – ribbons, depression, acrylic nails, football, class war, the sea – are somehow woven into a collection with a powerful unity of effect. Walker's style puts me in mind of a bowerbird, piece by piece raising something beautiful out of brightly coloured ephemera. Her voice pivots from deep emotional involvement with her subject matter to dissociated observation, and there are bursts of startling lucidity through the dreaminess; 'Waves swallowing friends and lovers like roman candles, / unaware I wasn't a system of caves.'

The collection's structure is cyclical, rising like a pendulum's swing through the twenty-one cards of the Tarot's Major Arcana, and then falling back through the same arc. A kaleidoscope can make the most familiar things extraordinary, and no matter how many times you rotate it, the same constellation never appears twice. Pass it to a friend, and they'll see something entirely different. Taking a look through *Kaleido* is much the same. Its pages are hot with psychedelic intensities of colour, musicality and texture; these are poems you can chew, hold up to the light or dig your fingernails into. A real sensory joy.

Out of these five pamphlets, *Flamingo* by Kathryn Bevis probably comes the closest to a conventional 'feminist' work – and yet it still strongly resists such lazy categorisation, all the while centring the pleasure and weirdness of femininity. The first three poems read as a triptych, like a portrait series of the same woman in different life stages. A slightly twee opening with 'Wonder Woman Questions her Status as a '70s Symbol of Female Empowerment' develops into two utterly stunning meditations on motherhood, 'Matryoshka' and 'In which I imagine my aborted foetus sings to me'. The nesting dolls whisper pityingly about their youngest daughter: 'born with no space / inside. That's right / She's wood all the way / through'.

Immediately after, the poet lends consciousness to her aborted foetus: 'i was your well-wound spool / your coil of line / that binds'. With this opening triptych, Bevis has crafted a portrait of female triple consciousness, deftly capturing an ambivalence about motherhood in our deeply natalist culture. *Flamingo*'s use of rhyme and regular structure is striking, given how unfashionable formality is in contemporary poetry, and yet these choices work perfectly for the collection's rhythms. The sudden eruption of cancer as a narrative priority towards the end of the book is startling, a rupture in its earlier thematic landscape. The poet makes it clear: the 'lemur' of breast cancer leaping through her body isn't hers alone, just as her body isn't hers alone. Her mother passed from the same sickness, and Nan-Nan also had a 'tumour nestling in her breast'. Bevis' achievement in these pages shouldn't be underestimated, *Flamingo* is a feat of putting healing words to open wounds.

Turning to *Tapping at Glass* by Tim Tim Cheng, I'm conscious that it's bad form to bring too much of yourself into reviews of other people's work but, sometimes, a piece of art hits so close to home that it is hard to stay out of frame. This collection deftly captures all the loneliness and alienation of the diaspora which I share with Cheng: 'The only correct analogy / between a city and your family / is when there's no return / but you still dream of home.'

Tapping at Glass is a breathtaking act of resistance against multiple violences – state violence, gendered violence, the geographic violence of diaspora. These are fragile poems, but written in a bold and resilient hand. The constant use of water and ocean imagery gives Cheng's collection a sense of boundless, restless potential. She maintains a strong authorial voice throughout, but always seems to speak for more than just herself. 'We mourn every day. We are good at it now.' 'A singer tells us: *we don't just scream / for suffering tonight. It's liberating, too. We release / / the wolves and thunderclaps within us.*' Even when writing in the first person, Cheng's presence in the text feels collective, polyphonic. If uprisings elected poet laureates, Cheng would be a strong contender for Hong Kong.

SZ Shao is a British Chinese landworker and artist based just beyond the London clay. She was invited to read at the 2022 Poetry Society AGM to represent The Poetry Society's work with young writers, and also participated in the 2022 Young Critics Scheme run by The Poetry Society and the T.S. Eliot Prize.

THE GEOFFREY DEARMER PRIZE

Judge: Niall Campbell

Where does one start when faced with such an array of different voices? For my part, along with the brilliance of the poem itself, I wished to feel that there was a sense of a poet getting into their stride. Some poems performed like Catherine wheels, exuberant but precarious, threatening to veer off course at any moment. Many, however, had the hallmarks of a poet ready to make their debut – Kaycee Hill, Kostya Tsolakis, Paul Stephenson, Charles Lang and Ella Duffy all stood out as possessing significant promise. The winning poem is JLM Morton's 'Lifecycle of the Cochineal Beetle, c.1788' (read the full poem on p.144) – a piece exceptional both in its poise and in its vivid metaphoric hold. The opening six lines are so carefully considered and perfectly lineated to draw the reader in.

As the epigraph explains, these insects hold colour. Small and potentially insignificant, they are to become central to fabrics and art – central to our places of power – but in a process that will cost them their lives. The lens of the poem never lifts too far from the nest. We are brought in close to the scientific particulars of its life, described with a vibrant interest. There are such beautiful phrases throughout – 'Holding her colour quietly in trust' – but only in the last couplet does the poem truly reveal itself. Pulling back to show the preparation to extract this bright crimson 'Destined for dominion.'

I love this ending. It situates itself between two readings – one where the insect is packed and travels as dye for the use of the high ranks. It is small – it will go to be used by those greater than itself. But I also perceive a second interpretation, where the insect, crushed and extracted, still achieves some strange victory by its splendour. JLM Morton has created just such a rich wonder.

Niall Campbell is a Scottish poet originally from South Uist in the Western Isles. His second book-length collection, Noctuary *(Bloodaxe, 2019), was shortlisted for the Forward Prize.*

Winner of the inaugural Laurie Lee Prize 2022, JLM Morton is a writer and educator based in Gloucestershire, UK.

The Geoffrey Dearmer Prize is awarded annually to the best poem in The Poetry Review *by a poet who had not, at the time their work appeared, published a full collection. The Prize was established in 1998 in memory of Geoffrey Dearmer, who at 103 was the Society's oldest member. It is awarded, through the generosity of the Dearmer family, to honour this noted World War One poet.* The Poetry Review *is extremely grateful to the Dearmer family for supporting this prize.*

JLM MORTON

Lifecycle of the Cochineal Beetle, c.1788

*'it is worthwhile recalling that from the medieval era, one
of the colours most prized by the crown, church and nobility
in Europe for their finest fabrics was that of carmine or deep
crimson.'* – Carlos Marichal Salinas

An egg breaks on the pad of a prickly pear somewhere
in Oaxaca where the scale insects' livid bodies

mass and crackle in the sun. Emerging, a crawler nymph
clusters with the softness of her siblings

to feed in the downy blanket – explorers edging
to the brink of the known world.

Nymph throws out a long wisp of wax,
a thread to catch a ride on the wind, lifting and

landing on the terra incognita of a new cactus pad.
Her claim is staked with a stab of her beak.

Cochineal sups the juices, sees off predators
– lacewings, ladybirds, ants – with the bright surprise

of her body. Fat, fierce and full of poison. She
has detached her wings. Has no need of legs.

Holding her colour quietly in trust – she waits
for the male to eat his fill, to mate and die.

Scraped away at ninety days, her body is laid out
to dry then pulverised. Destined for dominion.

CONTRIBUTORS

Kim Addonizio is the author of several books, most recently *Now We're Getting Somewhere* (2021) and *Bukowski in a Sundress: Confessions from a Writing Life* (2016). She lives and teaches Zoom workshops in Oakland, California. • **Sanah Ahsan**'s debut collection is forthcoming with Bloomsbury in 2024/25. • **Moniza Alvi**'s poetry books include *Europa*, *At the Time of Partition* and *Fairoz*. • **Caroline Bird** is a poet and playwright. Her sixth collection, *The Air Year*, won the Forward Prize for Best Collection 2020 and was shortlisted for the Polari Prize and the Costa Prize. Her selected poems, *Rookie*, was published in 2022. • **John Challis**'s debut collection is *The Resurrectionists* (2021). He lives and works in the North East. • **Jos Charles** is author of three poetry collections including *feeld*, a Pulitzer finalist, and resides in Long Beach, CA with her cat. • **Cortney Lamar Charleston** is an African American poet and the author of *Telepathologies* (2017) and *Doppelgangbanger* (2021). • **Courtney Conrad** is a Jamaican poet. She is an Eric Gregory Award winner and Bridport Prize Young Writers Award recipient. • Born in Nigeria, **Inua Ellams** is an award-winning poet, playwright and curator. His books are published by flipped eye, Akashic, Nine Arches, Penned In The Margins, Oberon and Methuen. • **Eve Esfandiari-Denney** was a recent UEA Birch Family scholar who is now beginning a PhD at Royal Holloway University in Creative Writing. Her debut pamphlet *My Bodies This Morning This Evening* was published with Bad Betty Press in 2022. • **Charlotte Geater** lives in Walthamstow and is chronically ill. She works part-time for Hackney Libraries and won the *White Review* Poet's Prize in 2018. • **Zuzanna Ginczanka** (1917–44), pen name of Zuzanna Polina Gincburg, was a Polish-Jewish poet of the interwar period. • **Sarah Hesketh** is a writer and editor. • **Katherine Horrex** lives in Manchester. Her first collection, *Growlery*, is published by Carcanet. • **Asmaa Jama** is a Somali artist, poet and filmmaker based in Bristol. • **Luke Kennard** is a poet and novelist who lives in Birmingham. • **Victoria Kennefick**'s first collection, *Eat or We Both Starve* (2021) won the Seamus Heaney First Collection Poetry Prize and the Dalkey Book Festival Emerging Writer of the Year Award, it was also shortlisted for the T.S. Eliot Prize, the Derek Walcott Prize for Poetry and the Costa Poetry Book Award. • An award-winning poet and poetry tutor, **Mimi Khalvati** has published nine collections, including *The Meanest Flower*

(2007), which was shortlisted for T.S. Eliot Prize. She is the founder of The Poetry School and a tutor with the Arvon Foundation. • **Prerana Kumar** is an Indian writer based in London. She was shortlisted for the *White Review* Poet's Prize 2022 and her debut pamphlet, *Ixora,* is out with Guillemot Press. • **Tife Kusoro** is a Nigerian-British writer and performer. As well as writing poetry, she also write plays for stage and screen. • **Rebecca McCutcheon** is a poet living on the Essex coast. She has recently had work published in *Propel Magazine.* • **Momtaza Mehri** is a poet and independent researcher working across criticism, translation, anti-disciplinary research practices, education and radio. • **Helen Mort** has published three poetry collections – her latest is *The Illustrated Woman* (2022). • **Jack Nicholls** came third in the 2020 National Poetry Competition and is the author of the pamphlet *Meat Songs.* He comes from Cornwall and lives in Manchester. • **Jeremy Noel-Tod** teaches on the Poetry MA at the University of East Anglia and writes 'Some Flowers Soon', a weekly poetry Substack. • **Kathleen Ossip** is the author of *July,* one of National Public Radio's Best Books of 2021; *The Do-Over,* a *New York Times* Editors' Choice; *The Cold War* and others. • **Michael Pedersen** is a Scottish poet and author whose books include *Boy Friends* (2022) and *The Cat Prince & Other Poems* (2023). • **Nina Mingya Powles** is a writer from Aotearoa New Zealand, currently living in London. She is the author of several pamphlets, zines and books, most recently *Magnolia* 木蘭. • **Deryn Rees-Jones** is Professor of Poetry at the University of Liverpool. She edits Pavilion Poetry. • **Padraig Regan**'s first collection *Some Integrity* was published by Carcanet in early 2022. • **Sophie Robinson** is a poet, novelist and nonfiction writer living in Norwich. She is the author of *Rabbit* (2018). • **Natalie Shapero** is the author, most recently, of the poetry collection *Popular Longing.* Her writing has appeared in the *London Review of Books*, the *New Yorker*, the *New York Review of Books* and elsewhere. • **Jessica Traynor**'s latest collection *Pit Lullabies* (2022) is a Poetry Book Society Recommendation and won the 2023 Lawrence O'Shaughnessy Award. • **Alissa Valles** is the author of the poetry collections *Orphan Fire, Anastylosis* and *Hospitium*, and translator of work by several Polish poets. • **Dawn Watson** was born in Belfast and is a lecturer in creative writing at Queen's University. She completed a PhD in poetry at the Seamus Heaney Centre in 2022 and is the author of pamphlet *The Stack of Owls is Getting Higher* (2019). • **Eric Yip** was born and raised in Hong Kong. He was the winner of the National Poetry Competition 2021.

THE Poetry Review

Space may be limited, book your place online at:
bit.ly/Summer23launch

The event will be hosted by *Poetry Review* Editor
Wayne Holloway-Smith

SUMMER ISSUE LAUNCH

Join us on Zoom 14 July 2023 at 7pm

THE**POETRY**SOCIETY

Supported using public funding by
ARTS COUNCIL ENGLAND

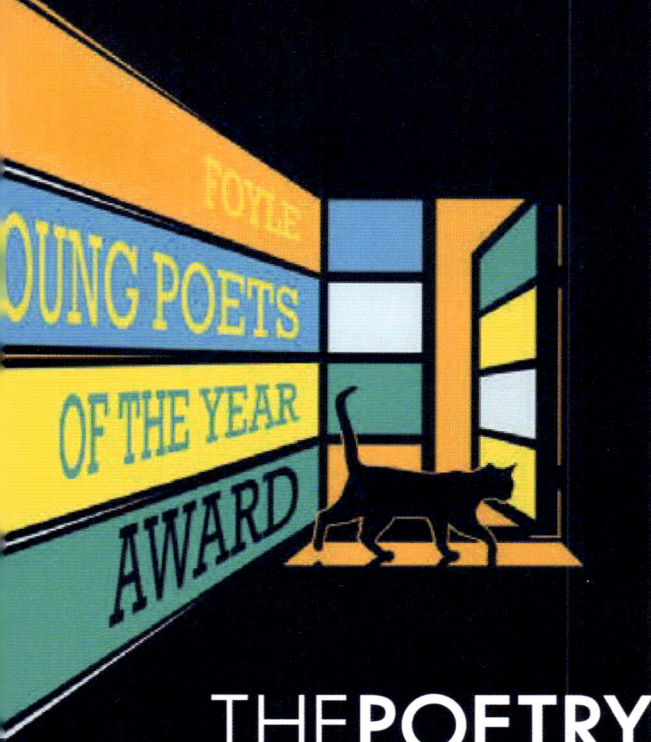

50 Years of *PN Review*

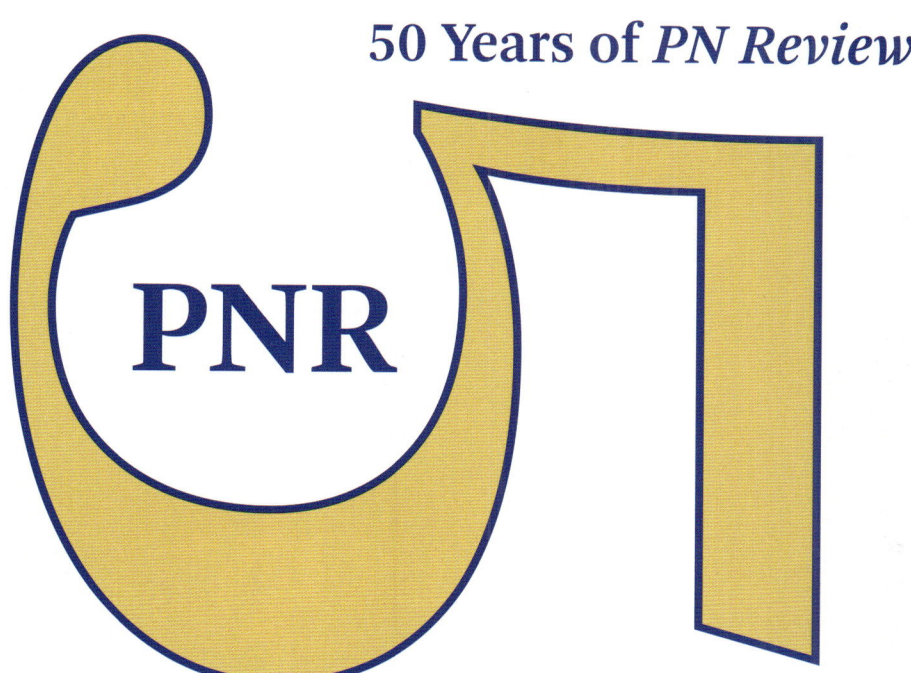

PNR

'probably the most informative and entertaining poetry journal in the English-speaking world' – John Ashbery

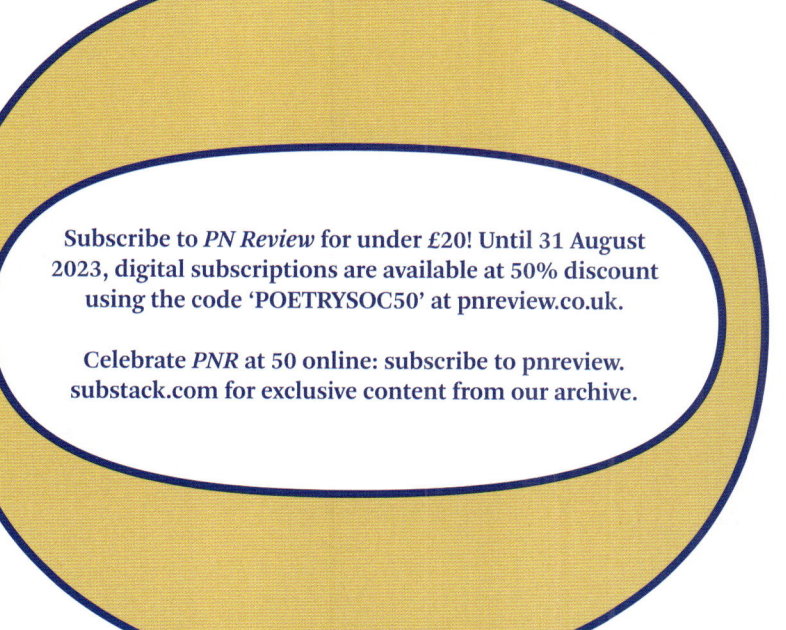

SOUTHBANK CENTRE

Poetry International

A festival of global eco-poetry and activism

FRI 21 – SUN 23 JUL

CAConrad
Ginkgo Prize for Ecopoetry
Jorie Graham
Gwenno
John Kinsella
Yang Lian

Cerys Matthews
National Poetry Library
Poetry Unbound
Olive Senior
Tongue Fu: Hot Poets
Belinda Zhawi

LOTTERY FUNDED
Supported using public funding by
ARTS COUNCIL
ENGLAND